THE TIME MANAGEMENT SOLUTION

---

21 PROVEN TACTICS TO INCREASE YOUR PRODUCTIVITY, REDUCE YOUR STRESS, AND IMPROVE YOUR WORK-LIFE BALANCE!

DAMON ZAHARIADES

ARTOFPRODUCTIVITY.COM

CONTENTS

OTHER BOOKS BY DAMON ZAHARIADES

The Art of Letting GO

Finally, let go of your anger, regrets, and negative thoughts and enjoy the emotional freedom you deserve!

How to Make Better Decisions

Fourteen proven tactics to overcome indecision, consistently make intelligent choices, and create a rewarding life in the process!

The Mental Toughness Handbook

The definitive, step-by-step guide to developing mental toughness! Exercises included!

To-Do List Formula

Finally! Discover how to create to-do lists that work!

The Art Of Saying NO

Are you fed up with people taking you for granted? Learn how to set boundaries, stand your ground, and inspire others' respect in the process!

The Procrastination Cure

Discover how to take quick action, make fast decisions, and overcome your inner procrastinator!

Fast Focus

Here's a proven system that'll help you to ignore distractions, develop laser-sharp focus, and skyrocket your productivity!

The 30-Day Productivity Plan

Need a daily action plan to boost your productivity? This 30-day guide is the solution to your time management woes!

The 30-Day Productivity Plan - VOLUME II

30 MORE bad habits sabotaging your time management - and how to overcome them one day at a time!

The Time Chunking Method

It's one of the most popular time management strategies used today. Triple your productivity with this easy 10-step system.

80/20 Your Life!

Achieve more, create more, and enjoy more success. Here's how to get more done with less effort and change your life in the process!

Small Habits Revolution

Change your habits to transform your life. Use this simple, effective strategy for adopting any new habit you desire!

Morning Makeover

Imagine waking up excited, energized, and full of self-confidence. Here's how to create morning routines that lead to explosive success!

The Joy Of Imperfection

Finally, beat perfectionism, silence your inner critic, and overcome your fear of failure!

The P.R.I.M.E.R. Goal Setting Method

An elegant 6-step system for achieving extraordinary results in every area of your life!

Digital Detox

Disconnect to reconnect. Discover how to unplug and enjoy a more mindful, meaningful, and rewarding life!

For a complete list, please visit

http://artofproductivity.com/my-books/

YOUR FREE GIFT

∽

I want to give you a gift. It's my way of saying thank you for your willingness to invest your time in this book. The gift is my 40-page PDF action guide titled *Catapult Your Productivity! The Top 10 Habits You Must Develop to Get More Things Done.*

It's short enough to skim but meaty enough to offer actionable advice that can make a real difference in your life.

You can get immediate access to *Catapult Your Productivity* by clicking the link below and joining my mailing list:

http://artofproductivity.com/free-gift/

We're about to embark on an important journey together. I can't promise that every leg will be immediately enjoyable. After all, there's some work involved. But I *can* promise that by the time we reach our destination, you'll look back with no regrets for having gone through the experience.

We'll be covering a lot of material that can revitalize and even transform your professional and personal life. The time management skills you'll learn will help create a work-life balance that aligns with your goals and priorities. It's a balance that should prove both gratifying and rewarding.

Onward.

NOTABLE QUOTABLES ABOUT TIME MANAGEMENT

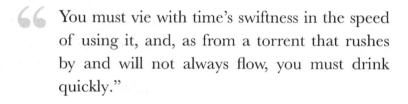

66 You must vie with time's swiftness in the speed of using it, and, as from a torrent that rushes by and will not always flow, you must drink quickly."

— SENECA

66 Lack of direction, not lack of time, is the problem. We all have twenty-four-hour days."

— ZIG ZIGLAR

66 You may delay, but time will not."

— BENJAMIN FRANKLIN

INTRODUCTION

~

Are you living the life you want to lead? Are you achieving goals that are important to you? Are you spending time with people who matter to you? Are you working on projects that fulfill you?

Your answers to these questions will stem mainly from how you manage your time. You're more likely to enjoy personal and professional success if you do it well. Manage it poorly, and you'll feel as if your circumstances are beyond your control.

Time is an equalizer. It levels the playing field. Each of us begins the day with the same amount of time. What we accomplish depends on how effectively we manage it.

Time: Our Most Valuable Limited Resource

Unlike money, you cannot re-acquire time after you spend it. Unlike enthusiasm and motivation, you cannot renew or replenish time after using it. Unlike a job, you cannot replace time if you lose it. Unlike the fuel you put in your car, you cannot buy more if you waste it, not through hard work, intelligent decisions, or crafty scheming.

Once it's gone, it's gone.

This unique attribute makes time your most valuable asset. It's the one resource you must protect above all others. When you treat time like a precious gift, you'll spend it where it will have the most significant effect and produce the largest dividends. Fail to defend your time, and you'll find that it slips through your fingers, never to be recovered.

On Being Vigilant against "Time Vampires"

Time vampires prevent you from making the most of your available time (that precious finite resource). They distract you, ruin your focus, and wreak havoc on your daily calendar. They torpedo your productivity.

You'll find them everywhere, and they come in various forms. At home, time vampires can include your television, phone, or neighbors who drop by unexpectedly. They might consist of low-priority emails, unnecessary meetings, or chatty coworkers at the office.

Time vampires can also be internal. These can include

perfectionism, fear, procrastination, and the inability to say "no" to others.

They are called time vampires because they suck the time out of your day. Left unchecked, they will suck the life out of your productivity. So you must be vigilant. You must protect your time from these "monsters." You'll discover how via the many tactics you'll learn in this book.

What Is the "Perfect" Time Management System?

The best time management system in the world is the one that works for you. I use many strategies to manage my time that you may find to be ineffectual. What works for you will depend on your unique circumstances, routines, and preferences.

For example, I'm an early riser. I like to work in the early morning hours. But you may be a night owl, getting your best work done when others turn in for the evening. I like to plan my daily calendar weeks ahead of time. You may prefer to plan one day at a time.

There is no universal time management system that works for everyone. Each of us is different, and our methods should reflect those differences.

This book will investigate dozens of best practices concerning time management. Along the way, we'll use these crucial building blocks to cobble together a workable, *effective* system that makes sense for you. This will be *your* time management system and no one else's. It will be the "perfect" system for *you*.

The Secret to Managing Your Time Effectively

If you don't feel you control your time, managing it well may seem like sorcery. You might think, "I don't have time to learn a system. I need a life preserver because I'm feeling overwhelmed!"

The good news is that anyone can learn to manage their time. The first step is acknowledging your time is precious and committing to making the most of it (we'll cover this in more detail later). Then, it's a matter of discovering what works for you and implementing those tactics until they become habits.

Good time management stems from good habits. Adopting the proper habits will make it easier for you to remain in control of your time, especially when life becomes chaotic. That's the "secret."

We'll take a quick tour of this book in the next section. Then, we'll dive into the good stuff.

Damon Zahariades
The Art of Productivity
September 2022

WHAT YOU'LL LEARN IN THE TIME MANAGEMENT SOLUTION

~

Time management is an organic process. Our ability to manage our time evolves as we learn about ourselves and recognize our strengths, limitations, and preferences. This is the reason your time management system will be unique to you.

I organized this book with two goals in mind. First, it should serve as a workshop. As we cover the material in the following pages, we'll slowly build your time management system from the ground up.

Second, rather than being a book you read once and forget about, it's a resource you can repeatedly revisit as the need arises. Wherever you are on your journey toward effective time management, you'll be able to find the tools you need when you need them.

How This Book Differs from Others

Many books that aspire to teach good time management skills have a common shortcoming. They offer sound advice but neglect to provide an opportunity to apply it in real life. The advice is helpful, but only on a surface level. There's little guidance regarding how to make use of it.

For example, these books might admonish you to avoid distractions but offer no insight on how to structure your environment to make this happen. Or they recommend you figure out where you're wasting your time but offer no instruction on how to do so.

I wrote *The Time Management Solution* with applicability in mind. You'll be able to read a chapter and immediately put the material to use. An exercise accompanies each tactic we'll cover to help you test and implement it.

Also, many other time management books make grandiose claims (e.g., "you'll gain two hours of free time each day if you follow these suggestions"). I make no such promises. Your circumstances are unique to you. Your results will also be unique.

My promise to you is simple: you'll receive the tools you need to build a time management system tailored to you wherever you are on your journey. Importantly, you'll be able to change this system as your needs, likes, and dislikes dictate.

A Quick Tour through the Time Management Solution

In **Part I**, we'll lay the groundwork. You may be familiar with some of this material. But we must start with a solid foundation that will support everything we'll cover later.

In **Part II**, we'll investigate the most common stumbling blocks that ruin people's ability to manage their time. This section may highlight issues you are currently struggling with, even if you are unaware of them.

Part III is the main section of the book. Here, we'll cover dozens of tactics and strategies you can use immediately to gain control of your time.

In **Part IV**, we'll examine how to manage your time when life becomes "uncooperative." Even the best time management systems can falter when challenged by unexpected situations. You'll learn a few essential tips on how to persevere.

I've also included a **bonus section**. More people than ever are working remotely. In this section, we'll talk about how to make the most of your time when no one is looking over your shoulder.

What to Expect as You Read This Book

We'll move fast through the material in the spirit of good time management. The chapters are brief and to the point. There are no fancy formulas with cute acronyms. No fluffy stories to "humanize" the topic. These are just useful, proven, *actionable* tips and strategies that you can start using today.

One last note before we begin. The exercises you'll find at the end of each section of Part III will help you decide if the proposed tactic will work for you. You don't have to do them all if you don't want to. Do the ones that you feel will be useful to you. You can do them as you read each section or wait until you've finished reading the book and then go back to do them later.

I'll provide the material, but you control how you progress through it. That is as it should be.

With that said, let's not waste any time. Grab your favorite beverage, roll up your sleeves, and let's get to work.

PART I

TIME MANAGEMENT
BUILDING BLOCKS

∽

Before developing a genuinely effective time management system, we must recognize and appreciate how time affects our lives.

How we manage our time determines how successful we are at our jobs. It influences how we balance our personal lives with our professional lives. It affects our productivity and what we accomplish and, in doing so, governs our sense of achievement. During stressful times, it dictates our motivation, prompting us to press on or give up in frustration.

In the following few sections, we'll examine the fundamentals of good time management. These are the building blocks. In the same way that our skeletal system gives our body structure and protects our inner organs, these building blocks will provide a framework for your time management system. They will help you use the individual tactics we'll cover later.

MANAGING YOUR TIME VS. BEING PRODUCTIVE

~

W e often think of time management and productivity as the same thing. But they are entirely different from one another.

Productivity involves getting things done. You are checking items off your to-do list. It's commonly believed that the more tasks you complete, the more productive you are (this is a falsehood that we'll discuss later).

Time management is about planning your day and scheduling tasks and projects with different — and changing — priority levels. It's about being aware that time is a limited resource and being driven to allocate it accordingly. It involves observing how you use this resource as your priorities change.

When we conflate these two concepts, we risk focusing on the wrong goals. Rather than organizing our time to best suit our priorities and obligations, we stay on the exhausting treadmill of getting more done at all costs.

Time Management Isn't about Time

Have you ever wished you had a few more hours in the day? Have you ever wondered how much you could get done in a 30-hour day? It's a natural craving, especially as your calendar becomes increasingly hectic and demanding. It also suggests that you're not making the most of your time.

Most people understandably think of time management as regard to time. How much time do they have at their disposal? How can they squeeze more time from their busy schedules? What healthy or enjoyable activities can they sacrifice (e.g., sleep, breaks, exercise, etc.) to gain more time in their day?

But time management isn't about time. It's about how we manage ourselves, given that time is a limited resource. How do we prioritize tasks and projects when there isn't enough time to complete everything? How do we respond to emergencies that wreak havoc with our calendar? How do we strategically adjust our focus as our priorities change?

A 30-hour day won't make our day any less hectic if we don't first learn how to make the most of that time. And that means learning to manage ourselves and our attention.

What Is Required to Be a Good Time Manager?

Most of the books, courses, and training programs I've seen that purport to make you a better time manager focus on scheduling. They teach you how to create and maintain a daily calendar, organize tasks into time slots, and plan your day when many demands compete for your time.

Effective scheduling is essential, of course. But it's merely scraping the surface of what is required to be an excellent time manager.

Just as vital is the continual cognizance that time is limited and, therefore, precious. This is easy to forget because time quietly slips by without calling attention. Its slow march often goes undetected. So we must train ourselves to notice and monitor it. Our constant recognition of time's limited nature limits our inclination to procrastinate and misallocate it.

Another skill essential to being an excellent time manager is the ability to reapportion our time as the demands for it change. This is easier said than done. It's also more complex than it seems. How do we reprioritize activities as their significance changes? How do we decide which interruptions warrant our immediate focus and attention and which can be ignored until a later time? How and when should we adjust our schedules to accommodate the demands we face?

Many people master the art of scheduling but struggle with these other skills. The tactics we'll cover in Part III will help you improve all of them.

Time Management as a Tool for Increased Productivity

Time management is, of course, directly connected to our productivity. It has an immediate and lasting impact on it. When we manage our time well, we get more things done that are important to us. When we manage our time poorly, we waste time on activities that mean little to us.

Effective time management makes us more efficient at whatever we focus our attention on. It improves our performance and lowers our stress. It boosts our confidence and helps us to be more decisive. It allows us to enjoy a healthy work-life balance.

These things make us more productive. Rather than merely staying busy, we can spend our limited time on things that are truly important to us.

Rather than thinking of time management and productivity as two separate disciplines, it's helpful to think of them as interdependent. They work together. The latter is nearly impossible over the long run unless we first address the former.

Next, let's take a brief look at some of the most common stumbling blocks to good time management.

ARE THESE STUMBLING BLOCKS PREVENTING YOU FROM MANAGING YOUR TIME?

∿

M any people who want to improve their time management skills mistakenly believe it's a matter of learning to set goals, prioritize, and keep a daily calendar. In truth, it's a matter of changing our behaviors.

Changing our behaviors is neither easy nor straightforward. Some of them are so deeply entrenched that changing them is extremely difficult. A lifetime of reinforcement makes it tough to let them adopt new habits in their place.

We'll explore the most problematic behaviors below. Our purpose is to acknowledge them and recognize how they impede your ability to manage your time. Once we accept their existence, we can start replacing them with better practices. We'll focus on doing so via the tactics and exercises you'll find throughout *Part III* of this book.

Note that the first couple of stumbling blocks high-lighted below are circumstances in which we have limited control. They are external factors. The critical thing to recognize is that we control how we *respond* to them.

Emergencies

When you're not vigilant with your time, it's easy to get stuck putting out fires all day. The time you would otherwise use to work on meaningful tasks is instead spent managing crises of all sizes.

There is a no surer, more predictable path toward burnout. And, of course, reacting to emergencies all day will ruin your efforts to manage your time.

Unnecessary Collaborations

Most companies encourage their employees to collaborate. In truth, such efforts can be beneficial. But collaboration is a double-edged sword. Left unmonitored, it can lead to time wasted in unnecessary meetings, responding to avoid-able emails, and having impromptu conversations about shared projects.

Pointless collaboration increases your time demands without increasing your engagement level. You're saddled with more responsibilities without an accompanying sense of ownership. This will eventually cause you to feel overwhelmed.

Lack of Organization

It's impossible to effectively manage your time over the long run if you're disorganized. Without a proper organizational system, things get lost, and it's harder to find them when you need them. You also become more likely to overbook your time, miss deadlines, and lose information critical to whatever you're working on.

Disorganization can negatively impact your physical workspace, daily calendar, and how you archive and retrieve crucial details. Doing so, it can wreck your time management program.

Inflexible Planning

This is the flip side of the coin of disorganization. Rather than playing fast and loose with your daily calendar, you run your schedule so rigidly that you leave little room for necessary adjustments.

This lack of flexibility prevents you from effectively responding — and managing — emergencies, changing priorities, and inevitable interruptions. While rigid planning gives you the feeling that you're managing your time, it makes it more challenging.

Speaking of interruptions...

Interruptions

You will get interrupted at some point in your day and likely multiple times throughout your day. It's unavoidable. Whether this happens due to coworkers, family, friends, neighbors, or the delivery man, count on it.

The worst thing you can do is immediately set aside whatever you're working on to deal with these interruptions. You cannot effectively manage your time if you do so. In Part III, I'll show you how to manage interruptions while remaining approachable.

Inability to Say No

Most of us have an innate desire to please others. It's a good, honorable trait. The problem is that some of us have such a strong need to do so that it interferes with our ability to manage our time. We automatically set aside our own goals, responsibilities, and workload whenever someone asks us a favor, requests our time, or hopes to delegate us a task.

We fail to set boundaries.

Whenever we say "yes" to others, we say "no" to ourselves. We commit our limited time and attention to others, depriving ourselves of these resources. We overextend ourselves, which wreaks havoc with our ability to manage our time effectively.

Procrastination

Many people believe procrastination is a time management issue. They assume it arises from an inability or unwillingness to plan, schedule, set goals, and allocate time accordingly. In reality, procrastination stems from issues related to *emotional* management. Anger, despair, low self-esteem, and fear (more on this below), among other emotions, get the better of us and discourage us from taking action.

The tendency to procrastinate can quickly become a bad habit. Once it becomes a habit, it leads to missed deadlines, lost opportunities, and wasted time.

Perfectionism

Perfectionism *can* improve your performance over the short run. It can help you to deliver high-quality work, motivate you to work longer hours and increase your level of engagement. But these tend to be fleeting gains. Over the long run, perfectionism imposes a net negative effect. It will cause you to obsess over unimportant details, needlessly complicate matters, and perceive whatever you're working on to be more difficult and complex than it truly is.

Perfectionists tend to have great difficulty managing their time. Their all-consuming attention to detail defies reasonableness and practicality. It prevents them from completing projects and causes them to miss deadlines. Perfectionists tend to suffer from tunnel vision, allowing essential tasks to fall through the cracks.

Laziness

All of us struggle with laziness on occasion. Show me the most productive person you know, and I'll show you someone who undoubtedly sometimes feels like loafing. Many things can cause us to feel lazy. Some are physical, such as a lack of sleep, exercise, and dehydration. Some are emotional, such as fear, shame, and low motivation.

Whatever the cause, laziness is a direct impediment to productive time management. It robs us of enthusiasm, joy, and pride in our professional and personal lives. We delay tasks, allow projects to go unfinished, and ignore our schedules and to-do lists.

Fear

Fear manifests in many ways, and some are difficult to recognize. We fear failure, success, and change. We worry about feeling embarrassed, suffering rejection, and being confronted and criticized for our goals, decisions, and values. We dread being unable to fulfill our responsibilities and meet others' expectations. Sometimes, we experience general anxiety and cannot pinpoint the reason.

Fear is a significant roadblock to effective time management. It erodes our focus, saps our energy, and destroys our confidence. Fear in all its manifestations makes things seem more consequential than they are, causing us to procrastinate and develop perfectionist tendencies.

There are, of course, many other stumbling blocks that

can prevent you from effectively managing your time. But these are the ones that tend to have the most significant impact.

With them in mind, let's now look at the resources you can use to counter and overcome them.

WHAT ARE YOUR MOST IMPORTANT RESOURCES?

∾

You possess a toolkit that will play a crucial role in developing and improving your time management skills. It's filled with tools that, if properly maintained, will help you to maximize your time. Once you've planned your day, scheduled everything on your daily calendar, and created the day's to-do list, these tools will help to ensure that you stay on track.

Given their importance, you must take good care of them. In the same way that a butcher looks after his knives, regularly honing and sharpening them, you must also look after these personal tools.

Your Energy Level

Whenever you work on a task or project, you deplete your energy. The more complex the issue you're working on, the faster the depletion. Once your energy has been drained and your stamina has been exhausted, it becomes difficult to focus. Distractions become harder to ignore. Your motivation and enthusiasm dwindle, making it difficult to perform at the same level.

Unlike time, which is a finite resource (i.e., once it's gone, it's gone), you can replenish your energy. You can make sure to rest, exercise, and eat well. Some people like to practice meditation. Some enjoy taking leisurely walks. The methods you use to maintain and replenish your energy depends on your preferences. I'll give you several ideas in **Part III**.

Your Emotions

Emotions have a more significant impact on time management than many people realize. If you're feeling sad, angry, bored, anxious, or resentful, you're more likely to think you lack control over your circumstances. Burdened with these negative emotions, managing your time effectively is challenging.

Conversely, if you're feeling inspired, hopeful, and happy, you're more likely to think that you can exert influence on your circumstances. You feel more in control. These positive emotions can move you to take purposeful action, make important decisions, and resolve issues that otherwise hamper your productivity.

You must look after your emotional health and monitor your emotional state, especially when you feel overwhelmed. Both can have a significant effect on how you manage your time.

Your Headspace

Constructive mind management is crucial to productive time management. If you look after your state of mind, you'll find it easier to focus, prioritize, and make the most use of your limited time.

While your emotions will affect your headspace, other factors have just as significant an influence. The good news is that you can control many of these factors. For example, research shows that an uncluttered workspace makes organizing and processing information more manageable.[1] Studies also show that you can improve motivation through self-directed rewards for reaching specific milestones.[2]

You can control these things. Doing so can significantly influence your mindset, strengthening your focus and reinforcing practices that support and encourage good time management.

Your Attention

You cannot effectively manage your time if you don't first manage your attention. The two are inextricably linked, and the latter must precede the former.

Attention management is about focusing on the right things at the right time. The challenge is that your attentional resources are limited and quickly consumed. So you have to allocate them with purpose and prudence.

You cannot control time. It will pass regardless of your efforts, intentions, and goals. You can only seek to *manage* time, making the most of the amount you have at your disposal. By contrast, you *can* control your attention. You get to set your attentional filters. To a great extent, you determine your immediate surroundings, exposure and susceptibility to distractions, and the tasks and projects you focus on at any given time.

Your Engagement Level

Engagement is loosely defined as our emotional and attentional investment in whatever is in front of us. When we're fully engaged, we're focused and motivated. We're more mindful of our immediate experience.

This state of mind energizes us, improves our mood, and helps us to perform at a higher level. We work more productively and enjoy a greater sense of accountability, purpose, and satisfaction.

We can manage our level of engagement by choosing

what we focus on (to the extent that this choice is within our sphere of influence). If we focus on things that are important to us, our engagement increases. This engagement makes us less vulnerable to distractions, better able to think creatively, and more likely to see tasks and projects to completion.

Your Time

Time is arguably the most critical resource you possess. It's not merely about having a lot of it at your disposal. It's about recognizing that your amount is usually less than you need or want. This creates a sense of urgency in how you allocate your time.

Ultimately, time is always limited and always fleeting. This being so, its allocation should reflect your goals, values, and priorities. This is easier said than done, especially when others pull the strings. Rest assured, the tactics you'll learn in **Part III** and the accompanying exercises are designed to help resolve this issue.

---

1. Sander, Elizabeth J., et. al. (2019, January) Psychological perceptions matter: Developing the reactions to the physical work environment scale. *Building and Environment*, vol. 148, pages 338-347, https://doi.org/10.1016/j.buildenv.2018.11.020
2. Woolley, K., & Fishbach, A. (2018). It's about time: Earlier rewards increase intrinsic motivation. *Journal of Personality and Social Psychology*, 114(6), pages 877–890, https://doi.org/10.1037/pspa0000116

WORK + FAMILY + PERSONAL TIME (I.E. THE BALANCING ACT)

~

Maintaining a healthy work-life balance is difficult, especially when life is busy and chaotic. The problem is that without such balance, you'll eventually struggle with burnout, low productivity, and negative emotions. These issues can wreck your ability to manage your time.

But there's good news. As difficult as it may seem to achieve an excellent work-life balance, it's entirely doable. You may need to adjust how you prioritize critical areas of your life. You might also need to modify or fine-tune your expectations (as well as others' expectations). But once you do so, you'll find it much easier to strike a healthy balance. And you'll reap benefits that currently seem out of reach.

Work-Life Balance Defined

At its simplest, work-life balance is how we juggle our obligations, responsibilities, relationships, and interests in our professional and personal lives. Good time management skills are essential to maintaining such balance (we'll discuss this in a moment).

When we achieve a good balance between work and home, we experience less stress and anxiety. We're also less susceptible to burnout and mood swings. Instead, we tend to act with greater purpose, engagement, and optimism. And as a result, we enjoy a greater overall sense of well-being. Maintaining proper work-life balance safeguards and preserves our mental health. It can even help to sustain our physical health.

The attention to work-life balance has changed over the last couple of generations. In the 1950s and 1960s, it wasn't treated as a priority. Workers remained with their employers throughout their lives and dedicated themselves accordingly. While doing so created a sense of stability in the workplace, it spurred many to prioritize their work lives over their home lives.

Today, much more attention is given to maintaining a healthy balance. This is for a good reason. The benefits noted above inevitably lead to a better quality of life.

Achieving Work-Life Balance through Effective Time Management

It is more challenging than ever despite considerable attention to maintaining a healthy work-life balance. There are so many demands placed upon us these days that we're forced to choose between competing obligations and interests continually. An hour spent at our job is an hour that cannot be spent with our loved ones. (And, of course, once that hour is gone, it's gone forever.)

Maintaining a healthy balance will depend considerably on how well you manage your time. If you know what you want to achieve each day and practice good time management techniques, you'll be able to sustain whatever state of equilibrium you desire. You'll be able to strike the perfect balance between your professional and personal life, confident that you're spending your limited and precious time in the most prudent way possible.

Quick Tips to Balance Work, Family, and Personal Time

Achieving a healthy work-life balance isn't the main focus of this book. While practicing good time management skills will naturally help you in this regard, work-life balance deserves its own book.

I've included a few tips below that you can start using today to master this balancing act. Note that most of them significantly affect how well you manage your time.

1. **Set time-related boundaries.**
   Communicate to coworkers, friends, and family members when you can address their needs and when you need to address your own. Be firm but kind.
2. **Master the art of saying "no."** This is one of the most potent skills you can develop. We'll talk more about this in **Part III**.
3. **Schedule breaks.** Breaks are crucial for maintaining your productivity, creativity, and level of engagement. But if you don't schedule them, you'll be less likely to take them.
4. **Plan your day on a calendar.** If you don't plan your day, you'll be more vulnerable to distractions, interruptions, and crises. (I use Google Calendar, but there are many good tools available. Use whichever one suits you.)
5. **Commit to a quitting time.** It's not always feasible, especially when deadlines loom and your boss is breathing down your neck. That said, it's much easier when you set boundaries and learn to say "no."

Finding a healthy balance between your work, family, and various interests is not only doable but essential. It won't matter how productive you are if you are burnt out, feeling stressed, unhappy, discouraged, and exhausted physically and emotionally.

Good time management skills are indispensable to maintaining this balance over the long run. In **Part II**, we'll explore the biggest time management mistakes people make today.

THE 7 WORST TIME MANAGEMENT MISTAKES

~

Most of us struggle with common roadblocks that counteract our efforts to manage our time correctly. Interestingly, most of these roadblocks are of our own making. We develop bad habits and unwittingly reinforce self-sabotaging patterns. These habits and patterns make it difficult, if not impossible, to stay productive while maintaining a healthy work-life balance.

If you're having difficulty managing your time, the reason is almost certain to stem from common mistakes. If these mistakes have become deeply-rooted habits, you may not even realize you're making them.

This section will investigate several everyday bad habits counterproductive to good time management. These mistakes are practically universal. Everyone makes them at some point. The good news is that all of them are under your control. If you're currently making them, you can change course and correct them. I'll provide helpful tips to that end along the way.

That's not to suggest it'll be easy. The more deeply a habit or practice is ingrained in the mind, the more time it takes to reverse and replace it. Just know from the outset that it's possible to do so. And the rewards make it infinitely worthwhile.

MISTAKE #1: NEGLECTING TO IDENTIFY YOUR VALUES

~

W hen life becomes chaotic, we lose sight of why we do things. Our attention is focused on the here and now as we struggle to put out fires, meet tight deadlines, and satisfy myriad demands.

But we must know our purpose if we want to live meaningful lives. Moreover, we should have absolute clarity regarding this purpose whenever we take action or make decisions. This clarity helps us to decide how to spend our time so it'll pay the largest dividends.

Determining our purpose requires a preliminary step: we need first to identify our core values.

Examples of Core Life Values

"Values" is a vague term often used without a precise definition. This makes it challenging to discuss values with specificity. Let's deal with that issue now.

Your values are the things that you consider to be important. Together, they form the moral code that informs your priorities and influences your decisions and actions.

They can stem from your upbringing. Or they might arise from your social life, culture, education, experience, or religion. Most people's values materialize over time from a combination of most or all of these things. Examples include the following:

- honesty
- integrity
- authenticity
- courage
- accountability
- kindness
- forgiveness
- self-control
- hard work
- thoughtfulness
- compassion
- learning

This is not an exhaustive list. Not even close. There are

dozens of personal values that you might embrace throughout your life. The question is, have you identified the ones that are important to you?

It's worth doing so. If you're unclear about your values, it'll be difficult to prioritize the demands made on your time.

How to Identify Your Values

The best way to determine your values is to ask probing questions and answer them honestly.

For example, ask yourself, "What have I accomplished that makes me happy?" Your answers might involve your job, family, or a side project you've been working on weekends (e.g., learning a new language). Following are other questions that will help you to identify your values:

- "Who are my role models?"
- "What recent actions have I taken that fill me with pride?"
- "What recent decisions have I made that make me happy?"
- "What recent experiences have made me feel fulfilled?"
- "What five things are more important to me than anything else?"
- "If I could do anything for a living, what would I do?"

- "What personal traits do I want others to associate with me?"
- "What inspires me to take action?"

You should now have a short list of your values. If you're dissatisfied with them, know that you're not stuck with them. You can change them at will. Personal values are rarely static. They tend to change over time.

The critical point is that your values define what gives your life purpose. This insight will guide your efforts toward managing your limited time amongst competing demands.

MISTAKE #2: MULTITASKING

∾

This won't be a surprise to you. Most time management experts caution that multitasking is one of the surest ways to hamper your productivity. It divides your attention and prevents you from focusing on any one task. This lack of focus ultimately hurts your performance and productivity. Because your attention is divided, you're less efficient and more susceptible to distractions.

Despite these drawbacks, society applauds multitasking. Those who appear to do it successfully are commended for doing so. Many assume that multitasking is *necessary* for success — both professionally and personally.

To be sure, some folks *can* multitask effectively. But they're in the extreme minority. At least one study suggests that only 2.5% of people can do so.[1] For the rest of us, multitasking does more harm than good.

Your Brain While Multitasking

Researchers have known for years that multitasking impairs our working memory.[2] Working memory is our ability to retain and process information in the short term. This is a problem because if we're unable to process information efficiently, we're less able to complete tasks efficiently.

Another problem is that multitaskers aren't doing multiple tasks simultaneously. It may *feel* like they are, but their brain is switching between tasks. It toggles back and forth, a process called "task switching."[3] The brain redirects its attentional resources from one activity to another.

Task switching is expensive in terms of cognitive efficiency. Researchers suggest that it might reduce your productivity by up to 40%.

So we know that multitasking is a terrible idea. It hurts your performance and reduces your productivity. This prevents you from making the most of your limited time. So how do we replace this practice with the single-tasking habit?

How to Develop the Single-Tasking Habit

We need to think of tasks sequentially. Rather than dividing your attention across multiple activities, focus on doing one thing at a time. Work on one job, complete it, and then move on to the next.

This sounds easy. But it's unlikely to be so, especially if you've been a lifelong multitasker. The good news is that anyone can make this change. All it takes is commitment and adopting a few simple practices. I recommend doing the following while you work:

1. Turn off your phone. Or at least silence it and put it out of sight.
2. If you're working online, limit yourself to a single browser tab.
3. Close your email.
4. Work in short bursts. Start with 10-minute sessions and gradually increase their duration as your ability to ignore distractions improves. Use a timer.
5. Take a short break after each work session.
6. Keep your workstation clutter-free.
7. Work from a to-do list.
8. Break down big tasks into smaller ones.

If you commit to doing the above daily, you'll slowly retrain your brain to work on one thing at a time. You'll gradually stop feeling distracted and stressed and become more focused and calm. Your productivity will improve. Your efficiency will improve. And you'll find it much easier to make the most of your available time.

1. Watson, Jason M. and Strayer, David L. (2010, August) Supertaskers: Profiles in extraordinary multitasking ability. *Psychonomic Bulletin & Review*, 17(4), pages 479-485, http://doi.org/10.3758/PBR.17.4.479
2. Redick, T.S. (2016) On the relation of working memory and multitasking: Memory Span and Synthetic Work Performance. *Journal of Applied Research in Memory and Cognition*, 5(4), pages 401–409, http://doi.org/10.1016/j.jarmac.2016.05.003
3. Schneider, D.W. and Logan, G.D., (2009). *Encyclopedia of Neuroscience.* San Diego, CA: Academic Press

MISTAKE #3: OVERCOMMITTING

~

I f you regularly feel swamped and overwhelmed, it might be because you take on too much. You overload yourself by committing to tasks and projects that shouldn't be on your plate.

You're not alone. We occasionally fall into this trap, mainly when we underestimate how long these tasks and projects will take to complete. But unfortunately, the consequences are dire regardless of our optimism. We start to lose focus, miss deadlines, and allow important items to fall through the cracks. We begin to neglect our health, skimping on sleep and nutrition in our increasingly frantic efforts to fulfill our commitments.

Eventually, we burn out. We feel defeated and become emotionally numb, both at home and work. This ripple effect negatively impacts our relationships, job performance, and overall quality of life.

Why We Overcommit

There are many reasons we take on too much (and suffer the consequences) for many reasons. One of the most common is that we can't say no to people. We agree to help others with *their* tasks and projects, even when doing so means abandoning our own. Ultimately, we end up with too many commitments on our plates. The inability to say no is such an important time management skill that I've devoted an entire chapter to it (ref. Tactic #10).

Another reason we overextend ourselves is that we always feel as if we're not doing enough. We think we can accomplish more, even when stretched to our limit. This feeling can stem from numerous factors, such as self-esteem issues, the desire for validation, and a longing to be seen as a high achiever.

We also overcommit because we're unwilling to delegate or trust others (we'll talk more about delegation in Tactic #11). We micromanage, fearing that delegating to others will lead to disaster.

Often, we become overloaded because we fail to prioritize the items on our to-do list properly. Everything seems urgent and vital, so we fail to allot the appropriate amount of attentional resources. This, of course, ruins our ability to manage our time.

Now we know *why* we over-commit. Let's talk about how we can stop doing so.

How to Stop Overcommitting

Correcting this behavioral pattern can be a long and difficult road when it springs from a negative self-perception. Issues such as low self-esteem and feelings of inadequacy demand a comprehensive discussion that lies beyond the scope of this book.

When the tendency to overcommit arises from other sources (e.g., unwillingness to delegate), correcting it is mostly a matter of developing the proper habits. I'm not suggesting the process will be quick and easy. But it is entirely doable.

First, be willing to say no more often. I won't belabor this point here, as we'll cover it in greater detail in Tactic #10.

Second, reassess your priorities. Some goals and outcomes are more important to you than others. But it's easy to lose sight of their prioritization, particularly when life becomes chaotic. It's a good idea to periodically revisit them to ensure that you're committing your time to things that matter to you.

Third, whenever you're asked to take on another task or project, review your calendar before you agree to do so. This will quickly reveal whether you have the available bandwidth. Simply pausing to reflect on your other commitments may be all you need to avoid overextending yourself.

Fourth, schedule personal time on your calendar. Create time blocks and treat them with the same gravity as you would a crucial meeting. When you see these time blocks on your calendar, you'll have a more realistic view of your capacity.

Fifth, learn to delegate. Delegation is a crucial time management tool. It protects your time and prevents you from spreading yourself too thinly. Done correctly, it also makes others feel that you trust them. This not only improves communication but also encourages *them* to trust *you*.

When you stop overcommitting, you give yourself the freedom to focus on your priorities. That means you can pledge your limited time to tasks, projects, and activities that align with *your* goals and desired outcomes.

MISTAKE #4: BEING A PERFECTIONIST

~

Years ago, I was a chronic perfectionist. I had convinced myself that it was the only way to be successful. It didn't help that many people in my life celebrated this mindset, discouraging mistakes at all costs.

I realize now how misguided I was about perfectionism. It prevented me from managing my time (more on this in a moment), and it arose from deeply seated personal issues. These issues went unaddressed until I realized how harmful my perfectionistic tendencies were to my performance and mental health.

Several factors can cause perfectionism. These vary from person to person, but see if you relate to any of the following:

- feeling of inadequacy
- the belief that your value is based on your accomplishments
- a childhood spent meeting others' high, inflexible expectations
- a childhood spent trying to please overly critical parents
- fear of others' disapproval
- fear of not living up to your past achievements
- feeling that you lack control in critical areas of your life

I struggled with some of these issues. But for a long time, I wasn't aware of them. It was only after I acknowledged my perfectionism and began to reverse the pattern that I was able to recognize and address them.

The irony was that I prided myself on my time management skills at the time. These skills were a mirage. I was fooling myself. It wasn't until I abandoned my perfectionistic tendencies that I realized how badly I was managing my time.

How Perfectionism Impedes Time Management

Perfectionists often have a difficult time completing their to-do lists. They become so focused on perfecting every detail of every task that their work is never good enough. And so tasks and projects are never finished.

I once spoke to an aspiring author who struggled with

this issue. He had spent years writing his first novel and hadn't yet published it. He always found ways to make it better (in his eyes). I believe he's still working on his book. He may never feel it's ready to be published.

Perfectionism also encourages procrastination. For some people, the compulsion to be perfect stops them from even *starting* projects. They become trapped in "research" mode, investigating every detail before moving forward. Or they procrastinate because they fear failure, which they improperly define as turning in imperfect work.

When we're obsessed with perfection, it's impossible to manage our time according to our priorities. Every task, from the trivial to the vital, becomes a monumental enterprise. Consequently, nothing gets done promptly.

If you struggle with perfectionism, don't lose hope. You can overcome it. Below, I'll provide a few tactics that worked for me. Perhaps they'll also prove helpful to you.

How to Stop Being a Perfectionist

The first step in overcoming any issue is to recognize that it exists and to acknowledge its harmful effects. People often pride themselves on their perfectionism. But they'll never truly defeat it until they admit that this predisposition is holding them back.

Second, think about times you've done things imperfectly. Ask yourself, "What severe consequences did I suffer as a result?" (The answer is almost sure to be "none.")

Third, think about times you've dedicated excessive

time and effort to do something perfectly. Ask yourself, "Given everything on my plate, was it worth it? Did I use my time wisely?" (The answer will probably be "no.")

Fourth, get accustomed to setting concrete limits on how much time you spend working on things. For example, give yourself 15 minutes to respond to an important email. Commit to sending the email after 15 minutes, even if the words you used are imperfect. The more you do this, the easier it'll become.

Fifth, whenever you are about to begin a task or project, ask yourself, "What is the end goal of doing this? What is the big picture?" This will help you pull back the lens and see the forest instead of being fixated on the individual trees.

Sixth, after completing a task or project, note the imperfections. Recognize that you could've perfected select details, but immediately ask yourself, "Would the time and effort required to do so have been a good investment given the big picture?"

Conquering perfectionism is mostly a matter of retraining the brain. It'll take time, so be patient with yourself. Know that with diligence and consistency in practice, you can do it. The upside is that you'll be one step closer to creating a time management system that works for you.

MISTAKE #5: IGNORING YOUR PRIORITIES

∽

Each of us has 24 hours a day. This might sound like a trite observation, but it peels away the falsehoods we tell ourselves (and others) when we fail to complete tasks and projects. I've lost count of the number of times I've used the following excuses:

- "I'm too busy."
- "I don't have enough time."

Of course, we all start with the same amount of time each day. Elon Musk, Richard Branson, and Jeff Bezos begin with 24 hours, just like myself. If I fail to complete things on time, the problem could be that I'm ignoring my priorities. Or worse, failing to prioritize altogether.

Our priorities tell us what is important to us. They

inform us how we should use our limited time when competing demands for it confront us. We can't do everything, so we must prioritize. That way, we can devote our limited time and attention to the things that align with our goals.

When we ignore our priorities or fail to identify them, we end up randomly allocating our time. That's a problem because there are usually more things to do than the time we have available to do them. Consequently, getting the *right* stuff done becomes a coin toss, a matter of chance rather than effective planning.

Consequences of Failing to Prioritize

Recall a day you worked frantically to address every item on your to-do list. There was a sense of urgency behind every task, including the small fires that happened throughout the day. You probably felt stressed as you juggled multiple jobs and projects. You may have even thought that you were losing control and your day was headed toward disaster.

This circumstance arises, in large part, from an absence of clear priorities. When we fail to prioritize, *everything* becomes a priority. Every task becomes critical. Every request requires our immediate attention. Ironically, this predicament prevents us from completing truly high-priority items.

This leads to another consequence: burnout. Scrambling to get *everything* done and failing to complete essential tasks and projects leaves us feeling overwhelmed and discouraged. We feel emotionally and mentally drained. And because we've been unable to make measurable progress toward our goals, we feel defeated.

When we fail to prioritize, we also become more inclined to react to events and stimuli that have nothing to do with our goals. Rather than planning our day and allotting our limited time to things that are important to us, we end up responding to *others'* priorities. This prevents us from taking purposeful, intentional action.

Setting clear priorities should itself be a top priority. With that in mind, the following are a few simple suggestions to help ensure you complete the things that need to get done.

How to Prioritize Tasks and Projects

First, I encourage you to use the Eisenhower Matrix. It'll help you to distinguish between tasks that are important, unimportant, urgent, and non-urgent. I'll explain, in detail, how to use it in *Tactic #3: Allocate Your Time Based On Your Priorities* (found in *Part III* of this book).

Second, highlight one item on your daily to-do list as your highest-priority task. If you complete only one thing today, it must be this one. Once you've highlighted it, tackle it before you work on other tasks.

Third, rate each task on your daily to-do list according to the amount of time it will require to complete. Assign a number between 1 and 5 to each task. One signifies a job that will require minimal time. Five means a task that will require a great deal of it. Making this estimation for each to-do item will help you to decide when to schedule time for them.

Fourth, be willing to reprioritize tasks as their importance changes. If a job becomes irrelevant, abandon it even if you've already invested significant time. You'll never reclaim the time you've spent. Cutting your losses and moving on to more important tasks is better.

Fifth, be realistic about the time you have at your disposal. There will be days when you'll have more things to do than time to do them. Be willing to abandon low-priority items or reschedule them for another day when necessary.

Prioritizing your daily tasks and projects will take less than 10 minutes. You can easily do it in the morning before you start your day. Or better yet, do it the night before so you can hit the ground running the following morning.

MISTAKE #6: CONFUSING BUSYNESS WITH PRODUCTIVITY

∽

Somewhere along the way, we began to conflate busyness with productivity. Being busy has practically become a badge of honor. Many complain, "I'm so busy!" but their complaint comes across as a subtle boast.

Many thrive on being busy, filling their schedules with unnecessary meetings, trivial tasks, and arbitrary deadlines. Rushing around and working frantically gives them an adrenaline rush. Although they accomplish little of any significance, the constant busyness makes them feel exhilarated.

All of us have experienced this predicament. We find ourselves working on things that are unimportant to us yet feel thrilled by the illusion that we're getting things done.

We're exhausted despite having made little progress toward our goals.

It's not always clear that we've fallen into this trap. So to improve our awareness, let's explore the differences between constantly busy people and those who manage to stay productive.

Busy People vs. Productive People

One of the defining traits of those who see merit in busyness is a lack of focus. Rather than advancing one or two high-priority items, everything is a priority (which is another way of saying *nothing* is a priority). Rather than working on a single task or project at a time, they work on several, juggling their attention between them.

Productive people tend to be exceptionally focused. They're willing to postpone or abandon low-priority items to advance their top priorities (which tend to be few). They work on one thing at a time, taking purposeful action after evaluating their options.

Busy people give the impression of being productive, but this impression is often a mirage. For example, they respond quickly (sometimes immediately) to emails, texts, and voicemails. They always answer their phones. They're always rushing to meetings.

Productive people recognize that responding quickly — or worse, immediately — to emails, texts, and voicemail can hamper their output and performance. They understand that responding promptly doesn't mean they must respond immediately. Productive people also know that answering their phones ruins their focus and encourages others to call more often. They realize that always being available shows poor time management and lack of focus.

Busy people always say "yes." Productive people are willing to say "no."

Busy people often have mile-long daily to-do lists. Productive people tend to create short lists of high-priority items.

Busy people are willing to skip breaks. Productive people recognize that taking breaks helps them stay focused, manage their stress levels, and improve their performance.

If you find that you're constantly busy, it's probably crippling your productivity and frustrating your ability to manage your time. Fortunately, this is a simple problem to solve.

How to Solve the "Busyness" Problem

I've already briefly mentioned a few of these suggestions. Their relevance here underscores their importance to the broader theme of time management. As such, we'll revisit them again and in greater detail later.

First, improve your focus. Admittedly, this is easier said than done, and I don't mean to imply otherwise. Sharpening your focus requires time and practice. But you can do some things starting today to achieve this goal.

For example, work on one thing at a time. When you

find yourself multitasking, consciously and immediately commit to single-tasking. Also, use time chunks to strengthen your focus "muscles." Start with short chunks (e.g., 10 minutes) during which you focus on one task or project. Gradually lengthen these time chunks as your ability to concentrate improves.

Second, eliminate distractions to the extent that you can do so. Learn to ignore those you're unable to stop. In *Part III, Tactic #7*, we'll create a structure for your day that supports this goal.

Third, assign a priority level to every task and project on your daily to-do list. Doing so will spur you to devote your time to items that matter rather than trivial tasks that needlessly consume your day.

Fourth, pick two or three specific times of day during which you'll check and respond to emails, texts, and voice-mails. Refrain from checking and responding outside these time windows.

Fifth, use a daily calendar alongside your daily to-do list. Seeing tasks and projects identified in time blocks on your calendar will clarify what needs to be addressed throughout the day.

If you practice these small habits each day, they'll eventually become part of your daily process. You'll do them without thinking. At that point, you'll have successfully overcome the busyness problem.

MISTAKE #7: BEING OVEROPTIMISTIC WHEN SCHEDULING THE DAY

~

Most of us are naturally terrible at estimating time. We tend to be overly optimistic.

For example, we presume tasks will take less time than they do. We take for granted that projects we've completed in the past will take the same amount of time in the present despite different circumstances. We stuff our daily calendar with back-to-back time blocks, neglecting to add buffer time. We wrongly believe that we can shift instantly from one activity to another.

As you can imagine, this tendency makes it difficult to manage our time. The consequences can be severe. We miss important deadlines. We fall behind in our schedules. We arrive late to meetings and appointments. In the process, we create needless stress for ourselves (and others).

This overoptimism has a name: planning fallacy. Most

of us occasionally fall prey to it. But if we aspire to master our time, we must learn to avoid it. The first step, as always, is learning to identify it.

Why We Fall Victim to the Planning Fallacy

Think back to when you were in school. Your teacher gave you an important assignment due weeks in the future. You estimated that you could finish it within a few days.

Days passed, and with the due date looming, you finally began to work on the assignment. As you worked, however, you discovered that you needed more time than you had initially planned. There was no way you could finish by the due date, and you were forced to ask your teacher for an extension.

Thanks to the planning fallacy, you underestimated how long the assignment would take.

Again, this happens to us all on occasion. We're naturally optimistic about how much time tasks require to complete. Sometimes, we overestimate our abilities and proficiency. Other times, we misjudge the complexity of a job or project. At other times still, we're overly confident about others' competency, availability, or willingness to help, others whom we must rely on seeing a task to completion. Or we presume things will go smoothly when myriad things can go wrong.

We're biased toward the positive, which causes us to misread these factors. When we misread them, we can't accurately estimate how much time a given task will require to finish.

Now that we're aware of the issue let's discuss how to overcome it.

How to Counter the Planning Fallacy

In 2000, researchers found that specifying when, where, and how we would work on tasks counters our optimistic bias, making us less susceptible to the planning fallacy.[1]

The researchers gave a writing assignment to two groups of people. The first group was instructed to set a goal regarding when they would complete the job. The second group was also told to do that, but to specify where and when they would write. The result? The second group tended to set more realistic goals regarding time to completion.

This practice has since become known as setting implementation intentions. That's a fancy way of saying we should detail our process toward achieving a goal in addition to setting the goal. In my experience, it works.

Another tactic is to break down projects into individual tasks. It's easier to estimate how long these individual tasks will take than to estimate the time required to complete the larger project.

For example, suppose you'd like to write a book. It's difficult to predict how long it will take to do so accurately. It's much easier to predict how long it'll take to write each chapter. Researchers call this the segmentation effect.

I've also found it helpful to be mindful of Murphy's Law: if anything can go wrong, it will. Things we cannot control will often interfere with our plans. It's better to add buffer time to accommodate such things than to remain overly optimistic and suffer the consequences later.

---

1. Koole, S., & Van't Spijker, M. (2000). Overcoming the planning fallacy through willpower: Effects of implementation intentions on actual and predicted task-completion times. *European Journal of Social Psychology, 30*(6), pages 873-888. https://doi.org/10.1002/1099-0992(200011/12)30:6%3C873::AID-EJSP22%3E3.0.CO;2-U

PART III

21 SMART TACTICS TO MANAGE YOUR TIME EFFECTIVELY

∽

We've arrived at the main section of this book. Thus far, we've discussed the core building blocks of time management (*Part I*). We've also investigated the most common mistakes likely holding you back from properly managing your time (*Part II*). In this section, we'll explore a diverse set of strategies that will increase your productivity and help you to build and sustain a healthy work-life balance.

Allow me to make three suggestions before we begin. First, you can read *Part III* in a couple of ways. You can choose the tactics you'd like to focus on, leaving the others for a later time. Or you can go through each one sequentially, reading this section like any other book.

The choice is yours. Do what feels right to you. Now

that you own this book, you can return to *Part III* at your leisure, heeding your needs and inspiration. As I've emphasized in my other books, you are the captain of your ship. Map your course accordingly.

Second, each section is accompanied by an exercise. I love doing exercises when they're included in self-improvement books. They help me to understand and appreciate the author's advice. Naturally, I recommend you invest the time to do the exercises at the end of each section in this book. They're simple and easy. Most will take little time for you to complete. That said, the choice is yours.

Lastly, consider *Part III* as you would the menu at your favorite restaurant. We're going to create something tailored to *you*. There is no one-size-fits-all time management system. Instead, our goal is to build a system suited to your unique needs, circumstances, and biases. I'm going to present a great many tactics. Some will undoubtedly align better than others with your interests, manner, and disposition. Feel free to focus on the ones that do so.

With those notes out of the way, let's get to work.

TACTIC #1: ORGANIZE YOUR DAY INTO TIME BLOCKS

～

Time blocking is a strategy designed to help us take control of our time, manage distractions, and focus our attention on a single task or project. Elon Musk popularized it, but many leaders and productivity experts practice it (or have practiced it), from Bill Gates to Ben Franklin.

At its simplest, time blocking is reserving time slots during which you work on specific tasks. Everything else on your to-do list is set aside during these periods or, ideally, given their own dedicated time blocks.

This strategy offers a lot of benefits. First, it will help you to prioritize your to-do list. When you assign time blocks to items, you'll be aware that there's only so much you can accomplish with the time you have at your disposal. This awareness clarifies what items should receive your attentional resources.

Second, time blocking discourages both procrastination and perfectionism. Every important task or project is given a specific time slot on your calendar. You'll know when you should start working on it. And you'll know when you must *stop* working on it so you can move on to your next time block.

Third, it discourages scope creep. This is a situation where a task or project changes while it is being worked on, growing beyond its original requirements. It is usually discussed in the context of project management. But it can happen on a personal level, too.

For example, have you ever decided to give your home a quick cleaning but spent far more time than expected doing a *deep* cleaning? That's a case of scope creep. Had you given the job a specific time slot, you would've been less inclined to allow the "requirements" to grow beyond your original intention.

Now let's talk about how to practice this time management strategy.

How to Time Block Your Day

There are four basic steps. Each one is simple but vital. First, take a look at your to-do list. Prioritize each item based on its importance and urgency. I'll explain precisely how to do this in *Tactic #3: Allocate Your Time Based On Your Priorities*. Note the priority levels next to each item on your to-do list. I use a numbering system from 1 to 5, with 1 signifying the highest priority. Feel free to use a lettering system (e.g., A through E) or any other method you prefer.

Second, estimate how much time each task will require to complete or advance it to a good stopping point. Note your estimations next to each item. These will inform the size of your time blocks.

Third, schedule your time blocks on your daily calendar. Whenever possible, arrange them according to your energy levels. I try to address high-priority items in the morning when my mind is clear, and my energy levels are high. I work on low-priority items in the afternoon when I'm tired, and my energy levels are low. You might work to a completely different rhythm. That's fine. The important thing is that you recognize it and create a schedule that aligns with it.

Your time estimations must be realistic. Be wary of the planning fallacy that we discussed in *Part II*. Rely on your experience. When in doubt, be conservative; allot more time than you believe is necessary. Doing so will give you a buffer if you need more time than you thought.

Be Wary of These Common Time-Blocking Pitfalls

Time blocking is a simple time management tactic. But it's easy to fall into common traps and make avoidable mistakes that will thwart your efforts to manage your time. Below, you'll find three of the biggest mistakes to be mindful and vigilant about. The good news is that all of them are easily preventable.

1. *Underestimating the time you'll need to work on specific tasks and projects.* Avoid this mistake by planning conservatively and using buffer time to compensate for contingencies and inaccurate estimates.

2. *Being inflexible with your time blocks.* You may need to shift your attention as your day progresses. If you consider your schedule immutable, you'll be less able to adapt to changing circumstances. Avoid this mistake by being willing to edit your time blocks as the demands on your attentional resources dictate.

3. *Neglecting to allot time for breaks.* It's tempting to disregard breaks as unnecessary, especially when they threaten to break your flow and hurt your productivity. Avoid this mistake by assigning time blocks for breaks. Don't just assume you'll take breaks when needed. Chances are, you won't.

∽

EXERCISE #1

Time block your schedule for tomorrow morning. First, think about every task you need or want to accomplish before noon tomorrow. Write them down.

Next, estimate how much time each task will require. Force yourself to plan conservatively and include buffer time.

Finally, plan your morning by assigning time blocks according to your estimations. I prefer to do this using an online daily calendar, such as Google Calendar. But for this exercise, feel free to do this on a blank sheet of paper.

If you have several tiny tasks to address, each of which will require minimal time, batch them into a single time block. Examples of such tasks include checking your email, making a doctor's appointment, or ordering a product from Amazon. Allot a 30-minute time block to complete all of these tiny tasks.

You don't have to follow the time-blocked schedule you've created for tomorrow morning. The purpose of this exercise is to practice using time blocks.

Time required: 15 minutes.

TACTIC #2: SCHEDULE EVERYTHING ON A CALENDAR

~

I've been using calendars for years to manage my time. I started with paper-based calendars in the 1980s and transitioned to online calendars when the internet gained steam. For me, they're an indispensable tool.

Calendars give me a bird's-eye view of my day, week, and month. Some projects, such as writing and releasing a new book, allow me to see several months in advance. I can easily schedule tasks and manage deadlines with an end goal in mind. And having a visual rendition of my schedule is invaluable.

Calendars also encourage me to limit the time I spend on activities. For example, I can block time from 6:00 a.m. to 8:00 a.m. to write, knowing that 8:00 a.m. is the stopping point. That keeps me focused and creates a mild sense of urgency.

And, of course, using a calendar makes me less likely to overcommit myself. If a friend or colleague asks for my help, I can glance at my calendar and immediately see available blocks of time.

If you're not currently using a calendar to schedule your day, I strongly recommend it. Don't be surprised if doing so makes you more organized and efficient, improves your productivity, and helps you to spend your time where it'll pay the most significant dividends.

Quick Tips for Using Calendars

Calendar management may seem intuitive, and a lot of it is. But there are a few best practices that'll help you to get the most out of them.

First, don't merely use them to schedule meetings, appointments, and events. Use them to block off chunks of time for specific tasks, projects, and personal activities. Note and monitor deadlines. Schedule breaks and vacations. Use color coding to distinguish high-priority items.

Second, use multiple calendars to manage different areas of your life. For example, I use one calendar to manage time blocks for my day. I use another to manage specific projects; these include to-do items and their respective deadlines. Specific jobs that have a lot of moving parts get their own calendars.

Third, create a color coding system that tells you, at a glance, the categories to which particular time blocks and tasks belong. For example, I use red to distinguish anything related to self-improvement (e.g., my weekly goal audits). I use orange to differentiate marketing-related tasks. And blue denotes birthdays, anniversaries, and the like. Tailor your system to your needs.

Fourth, share your calendar with all involved parties if you're collaborating with others on a project. This is easy to do with today's online apps (I'll highlight a few popular ones below). You can control the permissions for each individual. Restrict some to viewing access only, and give others, such as an assistant, the ability to make changes as needed.

Fifth, schedule buffer time for contingencies.

How to Use Buffer Time

It's a good idea to pad your calendar with buffer time. This is extra time that serves as a hedge for the unexpected.

For example, your boss might drop by for an impromptu chat. Or perhaps you work at home, and your dog gives you the "I need to go outside *right now*" look. These things aren't on your calendar, but you can't ignore them. That's the purpose of buffer time. It gives you a cushion to attend to unexpected developments without sacrificing the flow of your day.

Make use of buffers by allotting time before and after the time blocks on your schedule. The larger the time block, the more time you should allocate.

For example, suppose you've scheduled a short time

block (e.g., 8:00 a.m. to 8:30 a.m.) to read and respond to emails and return missed calls. Add five minutes to the beginning and end of this block. This gives you the latitude to manage minor interruptions.

Or suppose you've created a more extensive time block (e.g., 9:00 a.m. to 11:00 a.m.) to work on a project. Add 15 minutes to the beginning and end of this block. Your buffer should be more generous because you're more likely to experience interruptions during a larger block.

Buffer time is also helpful when you underestimate how long a time block should be. For example, suppose you've given yourself two hours to work on a project. But after two hours you discover that you need another 20 minutes. Your buffer time covers you.

Popular Calendar Apps and Tools

There are many calendar apps you can use to schedule your day. Some are simple, and others offer a variety of bells and whistles. Here are some of the most popular apps:

Google Calendar[1] - This is the one I use. It's simple, free, and platform-independent. You can sync it across your browser, phone (Android or iOS), and tablet. Despite its simplicity, Google Calendar is surprisingly flexible.

Calendar.com[2] - If you have a lot of meetings and appointments, you'll probably like this one. It offers scheduling features that are a bit more accommodating and easier to use than those in Google Calendar. Like Google's app, it's free and platform-independent.

Fantastical[3] - This one is only available for macOS and iOS. It offers many great features you won't find in simpler apps like Google Calendar. Despite these extra features, the interface is intuitive. There's a free version and a premium version. The latter costs a few dollars per month and comes with even more features.

Any.do[4] - One of the great things about this app is that it allows you to integrate your to-do lists and calendar. I love Todoist for managing my to-do lists, so I don't use Any.do. But a lot of folks love it. As with Fantastical, there's a free and premium version. It's available for Android, iOS, Windows, macOS, and as a browser extension.

Microsoft Outlook Calendar[5] - It's a little stodgy and outdated, in my opinion, but it's still a terrific calendar app. It's free and available for Android, iOS, Windows, macOS, and as a browser extension. If you use Microsoft 365, this one may feel especially comfortable as it allows a lot of cross-product integration.

We haven't scratched the surface regarding the sheer volume of calendar apps on the market today. I wanted to highlight these five apps because they've been around for many years, are easy to use, and are well-supported.

∾

EXERCISE #2

∾

SCHEDULE THE REST of your week using a calendar app. Think about your responsibilities at your job. Consider your obligations and commitments at home. Don't forget social engagements, such as coffee dates and get-togethers with friends. Then, create time blocks for all of them. Include buffer time for contingencies.

The purpose of this exercise is twofold. First, it'll help you to get accustomed to seeing your day (and evening) scheduled on a calendar. You might be surprised by how liberating it feels to know what you should be doing at any given time.

Second, it'll establish a scheduling habit. Once you form this habit, you'll want to start each day with your calendar. It'll feel strange to do otherwise.

I recommend using Google Calendar for this exercise because it's free and easy to use. But if you have a different app in mind, use that one.

Time required: 15 minutes.

---

1. https://www.google.com/calendar/
2. https://www.calendar.com/
3. https://flexibits.com/fantastical

4. https://www.any.do/
5. https://office.live.com/start/calendar.aspx

TACTIC #3: ALLOCATE YOUR TIME BASED ON YOUR PRIORITIES

~

Every decision we make and every action we take stems from our priorities. This includes napping, showering, and exercising to working on specific tasks and projects when our time is scarce. We decide what is important to us and proceed accordingly.

Sometimes this decision reflects our immediate needs or desires. For example, we feel exhausted and take a short nap. We feel famished and eat a quick snack. Other times the decision reflects our longer-term intentions. For instance, we aspire to publish a novel and devote two hours each morning to writing it.

Ideally, our priorities would be informed by our goals and values. When this is so, we feel confident that our decisions and actions are aligned with aspirations and outcomes that are truly important to us. Otherwise, we spend our limited time on trivial activities, including those that *appear* significant because they carry an air of urgency.

Important vs. Urgent

When we struggle with a heavy workload or mile-long to-do list, it's easy to fall into the trap of conflating two conditions that are often at odds with each other: important and urgent. We assume that urgent matters are important simply due to their urgency and warrant our immediate attention.

This is a problem for two reasons. First, the urgency associated with a particular matter is sometimes a mirage. Sometimes an issue isn't as urgent as it appears. You might know someone — a coworker, friend, or family member — for whom *everything* is urgent.

The second problem is that urgent matters aren't always important. They might be accompanied by looming deadlines and may even have an immediate impact, but that alone doesn't necessarily mean they warrant your prompt attention.

So to properly manage our time, we must be able to distinguish between important items and urgent items. The Eisenhower Matrix, a tool that aids our time management and decision-making, was explicitly designed for this purpose.[1]

How to Use the Eisenhower Matrix

Before creating an Eisenhower Matrix, we first need to define the conditions "urgent" and "important."

Urgent items always focus on the present. These are the tasks and projects with pressing deadlines. These are the minor emergencies and crises that excite and agitate others. They also include interruptions that threaten to disrupt your flow, such as incoming emails, texts, and phone calls. They demand immediate attention.

Important items align with our goals and values. These tasks and projects impact us in the present or future. We value them because they support what we want to achieve. Important items may or may not be accompanied by deadlines.

The Eisenhower Matrix encourages us to separate the tasks and activities on our to-do list into four distinct groups (based on the above definitions):

1. Important and urgent
2. Important but *not* urgent
3. Urgent but not important
4. Neither urgent nor important

Items in Group #1 deserve our immediate attention. There are clear consequences to ignoring them and clear benefits to addressing them in the present.

Items in Group #2 can be scheduled for a later time.

They align with our goals and values but are not time-sensitive.

Items in Group #3 are best delegated to others or set on the back burner to address when we have free time. These tend to be interruptions and have a minimal long-term impact on our goals.

Items in Group #4 can be ignored. They're distractions, neither time-sensitive nor pivotal to our goals.

Visually, these four groups are presented as quadrants. These quadrants appear in the following image.

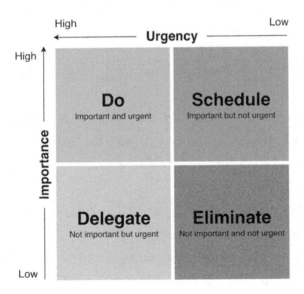

There are several methods you can use to prioritize tasks. These include the Ivy Lee Method, 1-3-5 Rule, and Warren Buffet's 25-5 strategy (among others). In my opinion, the Eisenhower Matrix trumps all of them. It's the most practical, helpful, and intuitive method I've practiced, and I highly recommend that you use it.

~

EXERCISE #3

~

LET'S CREATE AN EISENHOWER MATRIX. First, write down every task or activity clamoring for your attention. Include everything from major projects to phone calls from strangers.

Next, using the definitions we assigned to the conditions "urgent" and "important," write down "U" and/or "I" next to each item on your list. Some will warrant both. Some may deserve neither.

Next, assign each item to one of the four groups we specified above according to the letters ("U" and/or "I") you've written next to it.

That's it. You're done. You now have a clear picture of the tasks that deserve your immediate attention and those you can confidently schedule later, delegate, or disregard altogether.

Time required: 20 minutes.

---

1. The Eisenhower Matrix originates from a quote from former U.S. President Dwight D. Eisenhower: "I have two kinds of problems: the urgent and the important. The urgent are not important, and the important are never urgent."

TACTIC #4: PRUNE UNIMPORTANT TASKS

~

This tactic dovetails with Tactic #3. Once you can distinguish between important, high-priority tasks and unimportant, inconsequential tasks, you must decide what to do with the latter.

If you have a lot of free time, you can put them off, addressing them at your leisure. But if your schedule is packed and your free time is limited, it may be prudent to scrap them. Your free time might be better spent doing leisurely activities that help you to recover and reset your energy and focus.

One of the most efficient, effective ways to avoid feeling overwhelmed and burnt out is regularly pruning nonessential, low-value tasks. Decluttering your daily to-do list relieves pressure that otherwise causes you needless stress. Paring back the volume of tasks that demand your attention frees your mind to focus on *important* items.

If you created an Eisenhower Matrix in the previous section (Exercise #3), you've already isolated tasks that can be pruned without consequence or regret. It's then a simple matter of being willing to abandon these low-priority, low-value items.

This is easier said than done if you've developed a work ethic that compels you to complete everything on your to-do list. If you're a workaholic, abandoning them may even be antithetical to your ethos. So allow me to make a case for eliminating these unimportant tasks by highlighting the 80/20 rule.

The 80/20 Rule Applied to Time Management

Also known as the Pareto principle,[1] the 80/20 rule, as it relates to time management, asserts that 80% of our results spring from 20% of our actions. It's easy to overlook the significance of this claim because it is so often expressed as a fact of life. But consider its ramifications.

Take a look at your daily to-do list. If it contains 20 items, 16 of them are unlikely to advance your goals notably.

Review your client list. If you have 50 clients, 40 of them aren't contributing significantly to your overall sales.

Think about the meetings you attend each month. If you attend four meetings each workday (80 each month), 64 of them are probably a waste of your time.

Consider the articles you read each week to stay up to date at your job. If you read 40 each week, 32 of them are likely providing little insight.

Look through your closet at home. If you own 20 pairs of shoes, 16 of them rarely see the light of day.

These are simplistic estimations. But if you reflect on them, you'll find they're probably not far from the truth.

Applying the 80/20 rule, you can reasonably assume that most tasks that demand your time will have a minimal impact on your goals. It's worth asking why you should spend your limited time on them. If disregarding such tasks carries no consequences, eliminating them is best, preserving your time, energy, and attentional resources for more important matters.

4 Quick Tips for Eliminating Low-Priority Tasks

First, review your to-do list. Ask yourself why you're planning to complete each task. Are you doing so because you're responsible for it and it's vital to you? If the answer is no, mark it for possible elimination.

Second, think of every commitment you've made to others. These might involve projects you're working on at your job. They can also include social activities (e.g., participating in a softball league). Ask yourself whether a given commitment is a good use of your time. If it's not, revisit it with the person to whom you made it. It may be possible to pull out of it or reduce your level of involvement.

Third, note what you find yourself doing to avoid

other, more critical tasks. For example, you might check your email several times daily to avoid preparing a crucial presentation. You might test-drive productivity apps you have no intention of using to avoid working on a pivotal report. When you find yourself doing these things as an avoidance tactic, write them down for possible elimination.

Fourth, ask yourself whether a particular task or project can be delegated to someone else. This isn't just "passing the buck." Instead, some people might possess better tools, greater expertise, and more interest in a project than you. In such cases, it makes sense to delegate.

~

EXERCISE #4

~

THIS EXERCISE IS simple and easy, especially if you created an Eisenhower Matrix in the preceding chapter. If you did so, you've already completed most of the work. (If not, now is a great time to do Exercise #3.)

Review the fourth group of your Eisenhower Matrix. As a reminder, this group comprises tasks and activities that are neither urgent nor important. Commit to not spending time on them.

At the end of the week, review these items and note the consequences you experienced from ignoring them. Did you suffer a setback concerning your goals? Did your refusal to address these items create major interpersonal problems with coworkers, friends, or family?

This exercise is to help you grow accustomed to eliminating low-priority tasks, activities, and even commitments. It's to train your brain to think critically about everything you do and develop a willingness to abandon the stuff that has minimal value to you.

Time required: 10 minutes (at the end of the week).

---

1. This principle is named after Wilfredo Pareto, an Italian economist who noted that 80% of Italy's wealth was controlled by 20% of its population.

TACTIC #5: PERFORM A TIME AUDIT TO FIND "TIME LEAKS"

~

Our goal is to spend our limited, precious time on things that are meaningful to us. This can include broadening our skill sets to build our careers. Or it can involve working on something — at home or in the workplace — that makes us feel happy and fulfilled and give our lives meaning.

Unfortunately, we often spend our time on trivial things. We browse social media. We "shoot the breeze" with coworkers. We peruse the news. We check email 20 times a day. And along the way, we juggle meetings, phone calls, and other interruptions. It's no wonder we often feel exhausted yet unsatisfied.

All of us have time leaks in our day. Some are small; a few minutes dribble away here and there. Others are large and can waste hours. The worst part is that these time leaks often go unnoticed. And if we don't notice the leaks, we can't plug them.

We can solve this problem by performing a time audit. We can use this procedure to reveal how we spend our time. By tracking our activities, we'll determine whether we're using our time wisely or squandering it on pointless tasks, distractions, and other diversions.

How to Perform a Time Audit

We want to track how we spend time during a typical week. That being the goal, don't perform a time audit when you're on vacation — even if only for a day. Likewise, avoid weeks primarily devoted to a single activity (e.g., preparing a comprehensive sales presentation for a potential client). Instead, pick a week during which you anticipate doing things you usually do.

The essence of performing a time audit is to record the duration of every activity. This entails noting each activity's start and end time. You can do this using pen and paper or an online tool. At the end of this chapter, I'll share three time-tracking tools I've found perfect for these audits.

Here's what your audit might show during a couple of hours at your job:

9:00 a.m. - 9:20 a.m. — chat with coworkers
9:20 a.m. - 9:30 a.m. — use the restroom
9:30 a.m - 9:45 a.m. — check email

9:45 a.m. - 10:05 a.m. — browse Facebook, Twitter, and Instagram

10:05 a.m. - 10:30 a.m. — work on the weekly sales report

10:30 a.m. - 10:40 a.m. — chat with coworkers

10:40 a.m. - 10:55 a.m. — read news sites

10:55 a.m. - 11:05 a.m. — check email

Here's what it might show during a couple of hours at home:

9:00 a.m. - 9:15 a.m. — eat breakfast

9:15 a.m. - 9:30 a.m. — check email

9:30 a.m - 10:10 a.m. — browse Facebook, Twitter, and Instagram

10:10 a.m. - 10:20 a.m. — use the restroom

10:20 a.m. - 10:45 a.m. — respond to clients' emails

10:45 a.m. - 11:00 a.m. — clean the family room

11:00 a.m. - 11:20 a.m. — play Solitaire

11:20 a.m. - 11:40 a.m. — read news sites

Categorize these activities (e.g., meetings, phone calls, recreation, etc.). Doing so will make it easier to see how much time you spend on them during a typical week. You might be stunned by the weekly totals. But don't panic. This is the reason we're doing the time audit. We want to find the leaks that are going unnoticed. Once we find them, we can fix them.

What to Do after a Time Audit

After you've tracked your daily activities for a few weeks, review the results. Examine each category and think about the amount of time you devoted to it. I recommend asking yourself the following questions for each one:

- Am I spending more time than I imagined on this category?
- Which of the four groups of the Eisenhower Matrix does this category belong to?
- Is the amount of time I'm spending on this category warranted, given my goals and priorities?
- Can I reduce the amount of time I spend on this category and still fulfill my responsibilities?
- What would happen if I eliminated this category?

Identify your three largest time expenditures during the week. Do they align with your goals, priorities, and values? If not, they represent opportunities to prune and become more efficient.

Lastly, look for ways to reorganize your day to maximize your energy levels. Some activities may seem like a waste of time but may be well-suited for short breaks. Meanwhile, you may be able to reschedule high-priority activities to work on them during your most energetic, productive hours.

I recommend you perform a time audit every three or four months (or whenever you feel you're managing your time poorly). Otherwise, it's easy to develop bad habits. Regular audits will help you stay on track and show you where to make needed adjustments.

3 Time Tracking Apps for Running Time Audits

Time tracking apps show you how and where you spend your time. Their purpose is to help you to improve your productivity and efficiency. As you can imagine, some are better than others. The apps I've highlighted below meet three standards:

1. low cost
2. simple to use
3. intuitive reports

We don't need a lot of features. We need a straightforward app that helpfully provides information and insight. Here are three apps I recommend (you'll find links at the end of this chapter):

1. **Toggl**[1] - It's free and available on all platforms (Android, iOS, all major browsers, etc.). Toggl is painless to use because of its simple design. When you're about to begin a task, click the timer button. Click it again when you stop working. If you're using the Chrome browser,

Toggl will do this automatically according to whether your browser is open. The app knows when you're idle and will respond accordingly. This is great when you need to stop working to manage interruptions.

2. **ATracker**[2] - This one is available for Android, iOS, and as an extension for your favorite browser. Although there is a free ("Lite") version, it only allows you to track five active tasks. The paid ("Premium") version, which costs $2.99 per month, offers unlimited tracking. This app provides a visual dashboard with color-coded reporting. It also knows when you're switching between tasks. It's powerful yet easy to use.

3. **Clockify**[3] - Like Toggl, this one is free and available on all platforms. There are paid versions of the app, but they're unnecessary for running periodic time audits. Clockify is very user-friendly. It comes with a timer that you manually start and stop. And it presents information in a simple format.

Many other time-tracking apps will allow you to run time audits. Examples include Harvest, MyHours, Timely, and Timeular. But they're loaded with unnecessary features for our purpose — and often come with price tags that reflect these features.

~

EXERCISE #5

~

LET's perform a time audit for a typical day. You can do this the old-fashioned way with a watch, pen, and paper. Or use Toggl, ATracker, or Clockify. I recommend the old-fashioned way for this exercise, but it's your choice.

First, write down the activities you usually do each day. Refer to your daily to-do list, and consider items that aren't on your list. Examples of the latter include using the restroom, reading news sites, scrolling through Facebook, and eating lunch.

Next, create distinct categories for these activities. Think about how you'd like to see the information presented at the end of the day. For example, you might assign meetings to their own category so you can see how much time you spent attending them. But small recreational activities such as reading news sites and scrolling through social media might be assigned to a "bucket" category. You have a lot of latitude here.

Now, start tracking your time. If you're using pen and paper, write down when you start working on a particular task and when you stop working on it.

Finally, at the end of your day, tally up the time you spent doing the activities in each category. Add up the hours and minutes and write them down. Once you've done so, ask yourself whether your results reflect your expectations. Did you spend your time as you had imagined you would, or did you spend it in ways that surprised you? If the latter is the case, there may be an opportunity to make adjustments to manage your time better.

Time required: 20 minutes.

---

1. https://toggl.com/
2. https://atracker.pro/
3. https://clockify.me/

TACTIC #6: CREATE A SYSTEM FOR MANAGING INCOMING EMAILS AND PHONE CALLS

∼

E mails, texts, and phone calls consume a lot of our time. Worse, we often let them interrupt our day. We lack a system to manage them properly, so we end up in constant reaction mode, addressing them as they arrive. We feel strangely compelled to do so even though it ruins our focus and hurts our productivity.

How much time do we spend on email, texts, and phone calls? The answer may surprise you. According to a study conducted by the McKinsey Global Institute,[1] we spend 28% of our workweek reading and responding to emails.[2] According to data compiled by Statista,[3] we spend an average of five to six hours on our phones daily. And while some of that time is spent using social media apps, the amount is less than you might imagine (37 minutes per day[4]).

You don't have to remain a slave to your email and phone. You don't need to feel compelled to let them repeatedly distract you and interrupt your day. Below you'll find several practical tips you can use immediately to handle the flood of incoming messages while staying in control of your time.

10 Quick Tips for Managing Emails

We're going to move quickly through these tips. Some will no doubt be familiar or seem intuitive to you, so there's no need to belabor them. The key to making them work is to get into the *habit* of using them as part of an established system.

1. Select two or three times per day to check email. Do not check email outside of these pre-selected times.[5]
2. Check email during times of the day when your energy levels are low (e.g., right after lunch).
3. Set time blocks for reading and responding to emails. Start with 20 minutes. Adjust this time scale according to your needs. Once you find a suitable length, stick to it.
4. Archive emails that do not require a response from you. Don't delete them; you may need to refer to them later.
5. Get accustomed to ignoring emails that require no action from you. Over time, you'll be able to

identify by sender and subject line. Don't feel
compelled to read them. Archive them for later
reference.

6. Create folders and labels. You can do this
according to the sender (e.g., emails from your
boss, a particular client, specific friends, etc.)
and topic (e.g., weekly meeting recaps, company
newsletter, etc.).

7. Set up filters that automatically label incoming
emails. Create filters that automatically send
low-priority emails to the folders you've created
for them. Create filters that auto-label high-
priority emails with a red tag so you can find
them quickly in your inbox.

8. Unsubscribe from recurring emails you no
longer need. These can include newsletters,
group messages, and promotional emails from
businesses you've purchased products.

9. Keep your inbox clean. You don't necessarily
need to practice "Inbox Zero."[6] You want to
minimize clutter. If you've created filters to
auto-label and archive incoming emails, much
of this will happen on autopilot.

10. Create templates. If you send the same type of
email repeatedly (e.g., announcements,
newsletter, onboarding messages, etc.), use
templates to save time.

The goal is to create a *system* that revolves around the

above practices. Note that it's not necessary to implement all of them. Doing so may not even be possible, depending on your circumstances. Cherry-pick the ones that suit you. Test them to see whether they help. Keep the ones that do and jettison the rest.

5 Quick Tips for Managing Phone Calls

When our phone rings, it's hard to resist the temptation to answer it. This impulse springs from three sources. First, we're curious. Who's calling us? What do they want? Will I miss an opportunity if I don't take the call?

Second, we feel obligated to take the call. We want to meet the caller's expectations of us. We don't want them to be disappointed or upset with us.

Third, we want to be distracted. Maybe we're working on something we dread. Or perhaps we're trying to avoid work altogether.

The problem is that unless we take preventative measures, it's easy to fall into the trap of being servants to our phones. We instinctively reach for them whenever they ring. We inadvertently condition ourselves to do so.

Below you'll find five tips for squashing this impulse and improving your time management and productivity in the process.

1. Allow most calls to go to voicemail. Not only do callers tend to be more concise on voicemail, but you'll avoid interruptions.

2. Record a phone greeting that asks the caller for details. This discourages blind voicemails (e.g., "This is Ted. Call me back.").

3. As with email, select two or three times each day to listen to your voicemails and return calls (when necessary).

4. When you return calls, set the other person's expectations by politely asking, "I have five minutes. Is this a good time for you?" This will encourage the person you've called to get to the point instead of wasting time on small talk. If it's not a good time, plan a specific time to call back.

5. If you cannot reach the person you're calling, provide two times of the day they can contact you. For example, "Ted, sorry I missed you. I'm in and out all day. You can reach me at 11:15 or 2:45 this afternoon." This will help you to avoid wasting time playing phone tag.

You may initially find it difficult to resist the impulse to answer your phone when it rings. That's natural, especially if you've consented to this impulse throughout your life. But if you commit to making these five practices a part of your daily routine, you'll find it much easier to control your time.

EXERCISE #6

∼

THIS IS A TWO-PART EXERCISE. The first part involves email management.

First, look through your emails over the past 30 days. Note the ones that were important or required action. Note the ones that were unimportant or didn't require action.

Second, set up folders to hold future incoming emails based on the ones you've received. Then create labels that allow you to quickly identify them according to sender, topic, and priority.

Third, set up filters that auto-apply the labels you've created and auto-archive unimportant emails.

Time required: 20 minutes.

The second part of this exercise involves phone call management.

First, review the types of phone calls you typically receive. Who calls you? What is the purpose of the calls? Do you usually have to take action or provide information, or are the calls recreational?

Second, allow all incoming calls to roll to voicemail today. See whether there are consequences for doing so. (You'll likely find none or that the consequences are minimal.)

Third, schedule two 20-minute time blocks today to

listen to voicemails and return calls. Only return those that require a response (for example, ignore sales calls).

Fourth, when you return calls, tell the person you're calling that you have five minutes and ask whether this is a good time.

Time required: 15 minutes.

———————————————

1. Chiu, Michael, et. al. (2012, July 1) *The social economy: Unlocking value and productivity through social technologies.* Mckinsey. https://www.mckin sey.com/industries/technology-media-and-telecommunications/our-insights/the-social-economy
2. Note this study was published in 2012. While the data is dated, email continues to be a primary method of communication for business and personal use.
3. Statista. *How much time on average do you spend on your phone on a daily basis?* (2021, February) https://www.statista.com/statistics/1224510/time-spent-per-day-on-smartphone-us/
4. Statista. *Average daily time spent by users in the United States on mobile apps from October 2020 to March 2021, by category* (2021, October) https://www.statista.com/statistics/1272859/us-mobile-apps-time-spent-daily/
5. This may not be feasible if you have a job that requires you to respond immediately to emails.
6. Inbox Zero is an approach to email management that seeks to keep your inbox empty at all times.

TACTIC #7: DESIGN A STRUCTURE THAT KEEPS DISTRACTIONS AT BAY

∽

D istractions are inevitable. They occur regardless of our need to focus. They happen despite the work on our plate and the deadlines looming over our heads. It's not technically possible to avoid them. So we need a plan to keep them at arm's length. The good news is that we can create a structure for our day to minimize their effect on us.

The first step is recognizing distractions that threaten to sidetrack us. These vary for each of us according to our predilections. Some of us struggle to resist the lure of our phones while we work. Others can't help themselves from browsing social media. Many people have difficulty turning away chatty coworkers, neighbors, or family members.

These (and myriad other) distractions not only interrupt our flow and ruin our focus but can completely disrupt our time management efforts. However, once we recognize them, we can plan our calendars and create routines that keep them at bay.

Why Willpower Isn't Enough

You might assume that you can resist distractions through sheer willpower. This may suffice for short-term temptations, but willpower alone is never enough over the long run. The reason involves something called ego depletion.

Ego depletion is a theory that claims our willpower arises from a finite pool of mental reserves. We use up these reserves as we struggle to self-regulate throughout each day. We exert mental effort every time we try to delay gratification. Our reserves are thus steadily consumed, and our willpower declines correspondingly.

Eventually, our willpower dwindles to the point that we can no longer self-regulate. The distractions and temptations that promise immediate gratification overwhelm our ability to withstand them.

How to Distraction-Proof Your Day

The structure of your day should be tailored to resist and counter the distractions you struggle with. For example, disconnect your wi-fi if you find yourself repeatedly browsing the internet when you should be working. If you cannot focus because your day is filled with meetings, attend fewer meetings.[1]

Below are several other ideas that will help to distraction-proof your day. Some touch on ideas we've already covered in a slightly different context.

First, assign time blocks for essential tasks. Put them on your calendar. We discussed time blocks at length in Tactic #1, so I won't belabor the point here. I'll only add that these time blocks should be short enough to accommodate your ability to concentrate.

Second, check and respond to emails and voicemails at two or three specific times each day (Tactic #6).

Third, let others know you're not receptive to unnecessary interruptions during work-related time blocks. This is mostly a matter of setting — or resetting — others' expectations (we'll talk more about this in Tactics #9).

Fourth, if background noise distracts you, wear sound-proof earmuffs. It takes some getting used to, but once it becomes a habit, it'll seem like second nature.

Fifth, set aside time blocks for recreational activities. Many of us schedule work-related tasks on our daily calendar but neglect to schedule "play time" and self-care activities, such as exercise. Scheduling these things allows us to focus without being sidetracked by thoughts of when we'll fit them in.

Sixth, if you struggle to ignore your phone, use the 10-meter rule. Place your phone at least 10 meters away from your workspace while working.

Seventh, use a website blocker if you need to use the internet but find yourself wasting time on select sites (e.g., CNN, Facebook, Reddit, etc.). These blockers prevent you from accessing sites you choose for a specified period.[2]

Eighth, keep your workspace organized and free of clutter. Research shows that a messy workspace adversely affects decision-making, depletes energy, and increases stress.[3] In this state, you're more prone to distraction. Clear the clutter, and you'll improve your focus.

The idea is to develop routines and tailor your working environment to minimize the effect of the things that commonly distract you. Rather than relying on willpower to resist distractions, you can develop a structure for your day that automatically fends them off.

～

EXERCISE #7

～

WRITE down your most common time-wasters. They might include meetings, gossipy coworkers, or emails at your workplace. They may involve your television, the internet, and friends' tendency to drop by unannounced at home.

Next, brainstorm ways to counter each of the time-wasters you've written down. For example, if emails are a constant distraction, you can keep your email program closed while you work. If you have difficulty resisting the siren's call of the internet, you can turn off your wi-fi or use a website blocker. If your friends repeatedly make unplanned visits, you can politely ask them to stop doing so.

Now, implement one measure at a time. Once you've done so and can maintain it, implement another. This isn't a race. Give yourself time to apply these measures. Allow them to become habits. Where other people are involved (e.g., asking friends not to drop by unannounced), allow time to adjust their expectations.

Time required: 15 minutes.

---

1. Admittedly, this is easier said than done. But if meetings are added to your schedule because you appear available, fill your calendar with time blocks. This alone is sometimes enough to prevent others from adding you.
2. There are many good website blockers that are available for free. Among them are Friday, StayFocused, and Blocksite, all of which are available as Chrome browser extensions.
3. Roster, Catherine A. and Ferrari, Joseph R. (2019, January 13) Does Work Stress Lead to Office Clutter, and How? Mediating Influences of Emotional Exhaustion and Indecision. *Environment and Behavior*, https://doi.org/10.1177/0013916518823041

TACTIC #8: DEVELOP MONK-LIKE FOCUS

∼

Our ability to focus directly and often immediately impacts our time management. If we're unable to concentrate, even for short periods, we'll be less able to work efficiently and productively. Our capacity to accomplish important objectives while meeting strict deadlines will be crippled.

Talent, skill, and good intentions won't bridge the gap. Without focus, we're doomed to fight against the clock constantly.

Like ignoring distractions, many people believe that staying focused is a matter of willpower. They presume that they should be able to force themselves to concentrate, and if they're unable to do so, it means they lack resolve. This belief is an illusion.

Focus is a learned skill. It is developed over time. Like a

muscle, it is strengthened through deliberate practice and atrophies with neglect and nonuse.

Numerous factors work against us whenever we strive to focus. Our phones and other gadgets lure our attention. Friends, coworkers, and family members interrupt us and disturb our flow. Anxiety, stress, and lack of sleep deplete our energy; the less energy we have, the harder it is to concentrate. And, of course, the internet is a constant distraction.

We can take measures to counter these and other factors. It's a matter of identifying the things that most commonly distract us, creating habits that resist them, and practicing these habits consistently.

The Fundamentals of Focus

Our brain employs different types of attention to process information and resist distractions. One type is called selective attention. Here our brain attempts to screen out all stimuli except that related to whatever we're trying to focus on. An example is filtering the noise in a busy coffee shop while concentrating on what your friend is saying to you.

Another type is called divided attention. Here our brain attempts to multitask, splitting its resources to process information between two or more tasks. An example is talking to a friend on the phone while cooking dinner.

The third type of attention is called sustained attention. Here our brain devotes its resources to a single task over a prolonged period. An example is spending hours studying for a test.

Sustained attention is the one that has the most significant impact on our time management. If we can focus on one thing for an extended period, working on it to the exclusion of everything else, we stand a better chance of completing it. Without sustained attention, we risk flitting back and forth between multiple tasks. This wastes our attentional resources and all but guarantees we end up squandering our time on low-priority items.

Fortunately, we can improve our brain's ability to single task over prolonged periods. We can get better at it. Over time, we can develop this ability with a few simple practices and the willingness to do them consistently.

Focus 201: Best Practices for Improved Concentration

What follows is an assortment of tactics that have helped others to sharpen their focus. A few are universally effective. They work for practically everyone and are supported by scientific research. But some are effective for some but ineffective for others. So I recommend testing each one for yourself and recording the results. Maintain the ones that work for you and discard the rest.

First, create a morning routine. The purpose of a morning routine is not to get things done. Instead, it's to set the day's tone, help you to find your bearings, and start the day with a fresh outlook and peaceful mindset. Your routine will be unique to your preferences. Moreover, it may change over time based on these preferences and your circumstances.

Second, mind your energy levels. Work on tasks that require considerable focus (e.g., a year-end report) when your energy levels are highest. Work on rote tasks that require minimal focus (e.g., cleaning your living room) when your energy levels are at their lowest. We'll discuss energy levels in greater detail in Tactic #17.

Third, take breaks doing activities you enjoy. Take a nap. Cook a new dish. Enjoy a nature walk. Watch reality TV (we all have guilty pleasures). The point is that you do something enjoyable that gives your brain a chance to recharge and refocus. Research supports this practice.[12]

Fourth, create a workspace designed for productive comfort. If your chair hurts your back (or bottom), invest in a new, ergonomic chair. Or try a standing desk. If your neck and shoulders routinely become sore after staring at your monitor for 30 minutes, adjust the height of your monitor. The more comfortable you are while working, the easier you'll find it to focus.

Fifth, reduce the noise in your work environment. Wear soundproof earmuffs if you lack control over your environment (e.g., talkative coworkers, ongoing construction outside your window, etc.).[3]

Sixth, get restful sleep. A large body of scientific research shows that lack of sleep impairs our ability to concentrate.[45] For most of us, getting high-quality sleep is a matter of practicing habits that support it. Such habits include avoiding caffeine at night, keeping a regular sleep schedule, and putting our phones away an hour before bed.[6]

Seventh, break up your day into time blocks. We discussed time blocks extensively in Tactic #1. They are an invaluable tool for improving your focus. If you regularly have difficulty concentrating, start with 10-minute time blocks. During these 10 minutes, work solely on the task at hand. Then take a short break. Then do another 10-minute time block. As your ability to focus improves, extend the duration of your time blocks.

Eighth, regularly perform focus exercises. The purpose is to train your brain to concentrate. One such exercise is to resist the urge to reach for your phone while waiting in line. Instead, think about a problem at work and brainstorm solutions. Another exercise is simple meditation. Set a timer for three minutes. Sit down, close your eyes, and focus on your breathing. If you find your mind drifting to a particular problem, acknowledge it and pull your attention back to your breathing. Extend these sessions as your focus improves.

Ninth, avoid social media and current event news during the workday. Evidence suggests both consume our attentional resources and erode our ability to concentrate.[7]

Finally, maintain a healthy diet. It's no secret that certain foods (e.g., fruits and vegetables) have a more beneficial effect on our cognitive performance than others (e.g., donuts). Research supports this claim.[8] In short, if you need to focus, avoid the sugary stuff.

∼

EXERCISE #8

∼

THIS EXERCISE IS SIMPLE. Our goal is to strengthen your ability to focus over extended periods gradually. There are many ways to approach this exercise. Here, we'll read.

First, find a long-form, nonfiction article. I enjoy Long-Reads[9], but several online resources provide access to such articles (e.g., LongForm[10]).

Second, set a timer for five minutes.

Now, slowly read the article. Focus on comprehension and single-tasking. If your mind drifts while reading before the timer goes off, stop reading and reset the timer for another attempt.

Once you can consistently read without distraction for five minutes, increase the time on your timer to 10 minutes. Continue extending the time on your timer as your ability to focus on what you're reading improves.

Time required: 30 to 45 minutes

---

1. Howie, Erin Kaye, et. al. (2014, June) Acute classroom exercise breaks improve on-task behavior in 4th and 5th grade students: A dose–response. *Mental Health and Physical Activity*, vol. 7, issue 2, pages 65-71, https://doi.org/10.1016/j.mhpa.2014.05.002

2. Science Daily. *Brief diversions vastly improve focus, researchers find.* (2011, February 8) https://www.sciencedaily.com/releases/2011/02/110208131529.htm

3. Some types of ambient noise can actually improve our focus. This might explain why so many people find they can work productively and efficiently at coffee shops.

4. Alhola, Paula and Polo-Kantola, Päivi (2007, October) Sleep deprivation: Impact on cognitive performance. *Neuropsychiatric Disease and Treatment*, 3(5) pages 553–567, https://www.ncbi.nlm.nih.gov/pmc/articles/PMC2656292/

5. Miller, Christopher B., et. al. (2019, April 22) Tired and lack focus? Insomnia increases distractibility. *Journal of Health Psychology*, 26(6), pages 795-804, https://doi.org/10.1177%2F1359105319842927

6. If you struggle with chronic insomnia, "getting restful sleep" is obviously easier said than done. Overcoming insomnia is beyond the scope of this book and might require the help of a sleep specialist.

7. Lorenz-Spreen, Philipp, et. al. (2019, April 15) Accelerating dynamics of collective attention. *Nature Communications*, 10(1), https://doi.org/10.1038/s41467-019-09311-w

8. Klimova, Blanka, et. al. (2020, August 11) The Effect of Healthy Diet on Cognitive Performance Among Healthy Seniors – A Mini Review. *Frontiers in Human Neuroscience*, 14:325, https://doi.org/10.3389/fnhum.2020.00325

9. https://longreads.com/

10. https://longform.org/

TACTIC # 9: MINIMIZE INTERRUPTIONS BY OTHERS

~

Like most types of distractions, interruptions are a fact of life. They happen in the workplace as coworkers drop by to gossip and regale us with their weekend exploits. They occur at home as neighbors, friends, and family members call us on the phone (or worse, visit unannounced) to chat.

Interruptions impose a severe cost on our productivity and time management. Each time we're interrupted, our brain requires up to 20 minutes to refocus and recover our flow.[1] Even a single interruption each hour can have a detrimental effect on our ability to get things done.

Too often, we compensate for interruptions by working harder and faster and eschewing breaks. It's an understandable reaction. After all, we have to make up the time somewhere. But this "strategy" comes at a steep price: it increases our stress, causes us to make more mistakes, and contributes to exhaustion and burnout.

Fortunately, we can control interruptions both in the workplace and at home. It's possible to minimize them so we can stay focused and devote our precious time to the tasks and projects that require our attention. The first step is for us to identify the chronic interrupters in our environment.

How to Identify Repeat Offenders

The people who only interrupt us now and then generally aren't a concern. Exceptions aside, they value our time and don't mean to barge in while we work. In my experience, the interruption is usually justified based on the importance of what they want to communicate to us. (Or they didn't realize we were working in the first place.)

The problem is serial interrupters. These people routinely drop in to chat, seek help, ask our opinion, or waste time, procrastinating when they should be working. Their shenanigans ruin our flow and time management and can make us feel stressed and overwhelmed. We need to identify these repeat offenders. Only then can we take steps to manage their interruptions properly.

For this purpose, I recommend tracking the interruptions you experience throughout each day. Over the next two weeks, keep a log in which you record the following details:

- the name of the interrupter
- the date and time of the interruption
- the (stated) reason for the interruption
- how much time the interruption required
- whether the interruption was justified (from your point of view)

Some interruptions are valid, necessary, and even urgent. But most are not. To minimize the time-wasting interruptions, we need to distinguish between the two and identify the individuals who repeatedly stage the latter.

This log will reveal them. Over the next two weeks, you'll observe trends. You'll notice that some of your colleagues, neighbors, friends, or family members are guilty of interrupting you without good reason.

How to Insulate Yourself from Interruptions

You can use several tactics to reduce interruptions and minimize their effect on your focus and workflow. My favorite is the direct approach. When I had a corporate job, I used it to great effect. When colleagues dropped by unexpectedly, I'd say:

"Hey Brian, it's good to see you. I'm right in the middle of something. What can I do for you?"

The individual would get right to the point. And as you might expect, they tended to have valid reasons for subsequent interruptions. As a bonus, they never felt dismissed out of hand as I was giving them my immediate attention.

Another method is to designate a block of time each day (e.g., 9:30 a.m. to 11:00 a.m.) as "interruption-free" time. Then communicate to others that you must not be interrupted during this time block except for emergencies. Ask them to honor this daily time block.

You can also wear headphones. People will be less inclined to interrupt you if they believe you're listening to something (e.g., music, audiobooks, conference calls, etc.). They'll do so if they have a genuinely urgent matter that requires your attention. Otherwise, they're likely to move on. Note that you don't have to be listening to anything. Simply *wearing* headphones is enough to repel low-priority interruptions.

Another tactic is to relocate. If you cannot be found, you cannot be interrupted. At your workplace, try to occupy an unused conference room. Shut the door and pull the blinds. Passersby will be reluctant to disturb you. (Pro tip: make sure the conference room isn't booked when you intend to occupy it.) At home, if you're unable to work uninterrupted, pack your things and visit a local park, library, or coffee shop.

Simply closing your door can also ward off interrupters. If you don't have a door you can close (e.g., you work in a cubicle or your family room), post a "Please do not disturb" sign where it can be easily seen. Include a time when others can interrupt you. For example, if it's 10:00

a.m., post a sign reading "Please do not disturb until 11:15 a.m."

You'll notice that these tactics retrain others' expectations and behaviors. If you do them consistently, your colleagues, neighbors, friends, and family members will begin to respect your time and interrupt only when doing so is warranted.

∼

EXERCISE #9

∼

THIS SIMPLE EXERCISE employs my favorite approach for managing interruptions (described above). Over the next several days, whenever someone interrupts you, give them your immediate attention and ask, "*What can I do for you?*"

Asking this question is more difficult than it sounds, especially if you're unaccustomed to being direct with people (I know this from experience). That's the purpose of this exercise: to grow comfortable with doing so. The more you do it, the easier it will become.

Each time you perform this exercise, record the details of the interruption (wait until the person has left). You may be surprised at the trends you observe.

You'll gradually come up with ways to ask, "*What can I do for you?*" based on the person you're addressing. For example:

To your spouse: "Hey honey, I'm really deep in this job at the moment. Can I find you in 20 minutes?"

To a coworker: "Hey Bob, I need to talk to you, too. I'm swamped at the moment. Can we connect at 2:30 p.m.?"

To a neighbor: "Hey John, it's great to see you. I can't talk now because I'm in the middle of something. Are you going to be around in an hour?"

Again, this may feel awkward at first. That's understandable. We're naturally disinclined to upset people. But it's possible to do this with grace and respect. Moreover, if you regularly ask, *"What can I do for you?"* whenever someone interrupts you, you'll find that doing so quickly becomes second nature.

Time required: 5 minutes.

---

1. Mark, Gloria, et. al. (2005, April) No Task Left Behind? Examining the Nature of Fragmented Work. Conference: Proceedings of the 2005 Conference on Human Factors in Computing Systems, http://doi.org/10.1145/1054972.1055017

TACTIC #10: DON'T BE AFRAID TO SAY "NO"

~

Most of us are taught early on that saying "yes" is a respectable way to respond to others. When someone wants our attention, we're expected to provide it. When someone requests a favor, we're encouraged to be of service. That way, we show that we're well-mannered, courteous, and considerate.

But this lesson, which we learn as children, is rarely tempered with an equally important lesson that becomes crucial in adulthood: *It's okay to say "no."*

Our tendency to say yes is so profoundly entrenched from an early age that it's sometimes a knee-jerk reaction. Rather than arising from a genuine desire to help whoever is seeking our assistance, we say yes to avoid upsetting them. We dread turning people down because we don't want to disappoint them. Thus, we continue to say yes when we know intuitively that we should say no, given our other obligations, responsibilities, and deadlines.

It's important to acknowledge that saying no is often a legitimate response to requests for attention or aid. It's sometimes imperative that we respond in such a way. Because our time and energy are limited resources, we must allocate them judiciously. When we do so, we give ourselves the freedom to manage our time according to our priorities.

If you're a people-pleaser, saying no will be difficult — at least in the beginning. I know this from experience. The good news is that you can develop the courage to do it with grace, respect, and resolve.

Finding the Courage to Say NO

Saying no requires courage because we're naturally concerned with how others perceive us. We don't want others to think of us as unhelpful, selfish, or uncooperative. We want them to see us as accommodating, selfless, and approachable. The problem is that we allow this desire to frustrate our ability to say no when we need to.

To short-circuit this desire and dispel the fear of saying no, isolate the specific reasons that trigger this fear. Are you worried the person you're saying no to will become angry with you? Are you concerned that saying no will hurt their feelings or lead to a confrontation? Or perhaps you fear being regarded as lazy, ineffectual, or difficult to work with?

After you've identified the reasons that saying no fills you with dread, challenge each of them. For example, if you fear making others angry, remind yourself that you cannot control others' emotions. If you're worried about how others will perceive you going forward, acknowledge that others' perceptions of you are ultimately up to them.

Accept that you're not responsible for others' feelings, opinions, and attitudes. Let go of this imaginary duty and accountability. Doing so is a pivotal step toward developing the courage to say no with poise and determination.

How to Master the Art of Saying NO

Becoming comfortable with saying no requires awareness of our unhealthy triggers. For example, are we tempted to say yes because we feel guilty or selfish saying no? Are we desperate to meet the other person's expectations?

We must also recognize and acknowledge our limitations. For example, how much time do we truly have at our disposal? If we say yes to someone, will we still be able to meet our other obligations? Will saying yes require us to burn the midnight oil to fulfill our everyday responsibilities?

Lastly, we must retrain our brains. This step requires the most time since we need to undo years (perhaps even decades) of mental programming. This is mostly a matter of abandoning old habits that reinforced this programming and adopting new, healthier habits in their place.

First, whenever someone asks for your attention or assistance, ask yourself whether you have the time. Simply reviewing your calendar will reveal whether you do.

Second, establish time and schedule-based boundaries. For example, you might decide you won't spend your weekends on job-related projects (outside of rare emergencies). Or you may resolve to leave the office no later than 6:00 p.m. each evening.

Third, establish activity-based boundaries. For example, you might decide to refrain from helping people move, babysitting their children, or watching their pets while they're on vacation.

Fourth, brainstorm several ways to say no with finesse. This will help you to rebuff others' requests when you're focused, exhausted, or overwhelmed without triggering a confrontation.

For example, you might tell a coworker, "Sorry. I can't help you right now because I'm swamped. How about after 4:00 p.m.?" This informs your coworker about your circumstances and lets them know that you're *willing* to help but must do so later.

Or you might tell a neighbor, "I can't attend your party because of a scheduling conflict. But I'd love to attend the next one." This informs your neighbor that your lack of availability has nothing to do with them. Of course, don't lie. If you don't want to attend parties at your neighbor's house, say, "Thanks for the invitation. But I'd rather relax at home."

As with all habits, the more you do these things, the more natural they'll feel. Give it time. The upside is that learning to say no and doing it consistently will make it easier to manage your time and enjoy a healthy work-life balance. After all, saying no to someone is essentially saying yes to yourself.

∽

EXERCISE #10

∽

THIS EXERCISE AIMS to determine whether you tend to say yes for healthy or unhealthy reasons.

First, grab a piece of paper and a pen. Write down every instance where you've said yes to someone's request for attention or aid in the recent past. Take your time. Include small requests as well as large ones.

Second, write down why you said yes next to each item you've written down. For example, did you agree to help because it aligned with your long-term goals? Did you do so because you feared upsetting the individual? Did you say yes so that you could request a favor in the future (assuming the individual is willing to reciprocate)?

Third, think about how saying yes affected your time management. For example, did you need to stay later than you had planned at the office? Did you fail to complete every item on your to-do list? Did you miss any deadlines? Were you late in picking up your kids from school or baseball practice? Write down the productivity-based effect of saying yes next to every item. Where there was no effect, leave the space blank.

Fourth, for each instance, ask yourself whether you regretted saying yes. Hindsight is 20/20. What feels right at the moment often feels less under scrutiny down the road.

Lastly, review everything you've written down. For every instance when you said yes and regretted doing so, ask yourself how you *should* have responded to the request. Brainstorm the words you wish you would have used.

Time required: 15 minutes.

TACTIC #11: EMPLOY THE 4 DS OF TIME MANAGEMENT

~

One of the most common struggles associated with effective time management is deciding whether a particular task deserves our time. As I've stressed in this book, time is limited and precious. We must be prudent in how we use our time because the demands for it usually exceed the amount we have at our disposal.

The 4Ds of time management is a strategy that helps us to resolve this problem. It encourages us to make quick, purposeful decisions in how we tackle each task on our plates. It helps us to organize tasks and projects and prioritize them according to our goals.

The 4Ds are drop, delegate, delay, and do. They work together, giving us a simple procedure for ensuring important things get completed while helping us work efficiently.

Each task is scrutinized and assigned one of these four categories.

We'll talk about each of the 4Ds below. By the time we arrive at the end of this chapter, you'll possess a potent time management strategy you can use whether you're a student, freelancer, CEO, or retiree.

Drop

Some tasks aren't worth your time. Perhaps they fail to align with your goals. Maybe they're trivial and thus low in priority. Whatever the case, they can be ignored with minimal consequence. They can be "dropped."

An example is a promotional email you know doesn't require your attention. Another example is a meeting that has nothing to do with your responsibilities or the projects you're involved in.

In the preceding chapter (Tactic #10), we discussed how to say no to people and when to do it. This ability will prove instrumental in cutting out tasks that would otherwise threaten to ruin our productivity and time management.

Delegate

The ability to delegate appropriately is one of the most underrated skills we can develop. It's also one of the most beneficial because of the time it can save us. Unfortunately, delegation works counter to our natural inclination to control everything. For many reasons, from perfectionism to fear of being outshined by others, we like to do things ourselves.

The problem is that doing everything ourselves is almost always a terrible use of our time. It shackles us to small tasks, preventing us from addressing larger ones that need our expertise. At the same time, it prevents others from applying *their* expertise to these tasks.

When we delegate, we free ourselves to work on more critical items. This magnifies our impact on tasks and projects aligned with our goals and priorities. We also give ourselves more latitude to take advantage of new opportunities.

Developing this skill is beyond the scope of this book. Entire books have been written for that purpose alone. They address fundamental challenges, such as how to decide what to delegate and to whom to delegate it, how to establish performance benchmarks, and how to follow up on the outcome. For now, recognize that delegation is a valuable skill worth mastering.

Delay

Some tasks, jobs, and projects require your time and attention, but not immediately. They're essential but not urgent. They can be delayed according to your available time and the timeframe during which they must be addressed or completed.

For example, suppose you receive an email from your

boss. They want you to prepare a particular report and request that you deliver it in three weeks. If you know the report will take one week to complete and have other urgent items to address, you can postpone working on it.

Or suppose you need to take your car into the shop for a routine oil change. It's an important task because regularly changing the oil will help keep your vehicle in good shape. But it's probably (hopefully) not an *urgent* task. You can delay it for a few days without consequence and address it on the weekend.

Do

This last "D" is typically reserved for important and urgent tasks. These are the ones that demand your immediate attention. There are consequences for ignoring or delaying them, and possibly delegating them.

An example is your boss requesting your immediate help on a high-priority item within your area of expertise. Ignoring the request or delaying your response could anger your boss and negatively affect your performance review. So you must take immediate action.

Another example is getting a flat tire. You can't ignore the flat. You can't postpone taking action to fix it. It's possible to delegate it to a repair shop, but you must arrange to have a tow truck deliver your car to the shop. In other words, you must take immediate action.

In addition to important, urgent tasks, I recommend assigning small tasks that can be completed in a couple of minutes to this last "D." For example, suppose you receive an important email but not urgent. If you can respond to the email within a minute or two, it's best to do so now rather than postpone it.

∼

EXERCISE #11

∼

Do you remember the Eisenhower Matrix that we created in Exercise #3? We're going to use that Matrix for this exercise.

If you skipped Exercise #3, we'll need to create an Eisenhower Matrix from scratch. Don't worry. We can do so quickly and easily. Refer to the instructions in that exercise. For our purpose here, your Matrix doesn't have to be comprehensive. There's no need to include every item currently demanding your attention. We merely want your Matrix to include at least *one* item for each of the 4Ds described above.

If you already created your Eisenhower Matrix during Exercise #3, *this* exercise will be primarily one of observation.

Examine your Matrix. It should include the following four groups or quadrants:

1. Important and urgent

2. Important but *not* urgent
3. Urgent but not important
4. Neither urgent nor important

Note that the tasks assigned to the first group of your Eisenhower Matrix (i.e., "important and urgent") would naturally be assigned to the "Do" category of the 4Ds of time management. These are the ones that demand immediate action.

The tasks assigned to the second group of your Matrix would be assigned to the "Delay" category of the 4Ds.

The tasks assigned to the third group of your Matrix could be assigned to the "Delegate" category of the 4Ds.

And finally, the tasks assigned to the fourth group of your Matrix would be assigned to the "Drop" category of the 4Ds.

This exercise aims to note how the 4Ds of time management coincide with the four groups (or quadrants) of the Eisenhower Matrix. They serve a similar purpose but employ different methodologies and are presented somewhat differently.

I recommend using both approaches, at least until you decide which one you prefer. Using both time management frameworks will reinforce the necessity of prioritization and encourage you to develop the habit.

Time required: 10 minutes.

TACTIC #12: TAKE ADVANTAGE OF TIME BATCHING

❧

To-do lists are indispensable when it comes to getting things done. They make us more efficient and productive. They keep us focused. They can even help us to stay motivated as our energy levels wane. They're so crucial to time management that we'll spend an entire chapter discussing them (Tactic #18).

I mention them here because people often make them too long, hampering their effectiveness. It's a common mistake because we have so many things that we need to address each day. Consequently, our to-do lists become mile-long *wish* lists filled with minutiae instead of focused lists composed of our highest-priority, highest-value tasks. It's no wonder that so many of us fail to complete them.

Fortunately, you can use a simple solution to avoid this

pitfall: task batching. It's so simple that there's no learning curve. You can start using it today.

Time Batching Explained

The essence of time batching is that you group similar tasks and work on them during a single work session. We work on them for a specified time (i.e., time block) without interruption. Because these tasks are similar in scope, complexity, and outcome, we're more efficient and productive while working on them. We experience flow.

For example, imagine addressing emails as they arrive in your inbox. Whenever your email program alerts you of an incoming email, you drop whatever you're working on to read and respond to it. These emails become a continual distraction. They erode your focus and break your flow.

Now imagine setting aside 30 minutes twice daily to address emails (e.g., 9:30 a.m. and 2:30 p.m.). All of your attentional resources are devoted to this singular task. You're no longer multitasking. You're no longer repeatedly interrupted, pulled away from other duties to perform this on a piecemeal basis. You avoid the steep costs associated with task switching.

This is time-batching in a nutshell. It's a useful time management technique because it's easy to implement and yields immediate dividends. It's also flexible enough to use at home and in the workplace.

For example, think of the household chores that need your attention. Examples might include the following:

- vacuum the rooms
- change bed sheets
- wash the dishes
- wipe down the windows
- dust the furniture
- prepare dinner
- do the laundry
- take out the trash
- scrub the showers
- declutter the fridge
- throw out old clothes
- organize the closets

You can time batch some of these tasks to increase your efficiency. For instance, changing the bed sheets and doing the laundry go together. Throwing out old clothes and organizing your closets go together. Decluttering your refrigerator and taking out the trash also pair well.

Whether you use time batching at home or in the office, the point is that it allows you to focus. That, in turn, improves your productivity, making you less likely to waste time.

As a bonus, it'll also help you to avoid creating to-do lists that are too long and consequently fruitless. Instead, batch similar tasks as part of the same project (e.g., "Respond to Emails/Texts/Phone Calls," "Organize Closets," etc.) and add the project as a single line item.

4 Quick Tips for Effective Time Batching

As mentioned above, time batching is a simple yet powerful time management strategy. A few quick tips will help you to get maximum mileage from it.

First, look for opportunities to group dissimilar tasks when doing so makes sense. For example, if you're picking up your kids from school and your car needs gas, batch these tasks and take care of them during the same outing. Remember, there are no "rules" to time batching. There are only guidelines that you can adjust to suit your needs.

Second, assign time blocks during which you intend to address the tasks you've batched together. Place these time blocks on your calendar, so they're a part of your schedule.

Third, take steps to eliminate distractions. Time batching already offers a buffer against distractions that stem from task switching. But you can take it a step further. For example, turn off your phone, so you won't be interrupted by its audible notifications. Inform your coworkers (or family members or roommates if you're working at home) that you need to work undisturbed for the next 30 minutes.

Fourth, after each time-batching session, evaluate your performance. Were you able to complete tasks more quickly than if you had addressed them in a haphazard, piecemeal fashion? Did you feel focused while working on them? Were you able to ignore distractions? Did you batch tasks correctly? What changes should you make to produce better results from future sessions?

Although you can (and should) use this time management tactic immediately, learning to use it effectively is still a process. But once you optimize it according to your circumstances, you'll return to it repeatedly.

~

EXERCISE #12

~

FIRST, create a list of every task you need to complete. If possible, do this on your computer, as doing so will make it easy to organize these tasks in various ways (alphabetically, by function, by complexity, etc.).

Second, review your list and look for items that pair well based on scope and outcome. For example, responding to emails and voicemails are similar concerning both criteria. Likewise, doing the laundry and changing the bed sheets.

Third, assign a reasonable amount of time to address tasks once you've grouped them. You don't need to be perfect. Make an estimation. You can adjust it from experience down the road.

Fourth, tackle the grouped tasks. Work toward completing them in a distraction-free environment.

Fifth, evaluate the session. Did you set aside enough time? Were some tasks, in retrospect, grouped poorly? Did you experience distractions that you can eliminate in the future?

Each time you perform this exercise, you'll improve your ability to pair tasks and assign adequate time blocks. It's a practice that you'll optimize with time and experience.

Time required (steps 1 - 3 and 5): 20 minutes.

Time required (step 4): Varies

TACTIC #13: MAKE THE MOST OF
UNSCHEDULED DOWNTIME

～

Despite our best intentions, time slips through our
fingers each day. It's not always because of poor
scheduling, openness to distractions, procrastination, or lack of motivation. There are myriad reasons
that unscheduled downtime occurs, and it doesn't necessarily indicate a failure in time management.

For example, imagine arriving on time for a meeting
but learning that a key project team member is running
late. You might feel compelled to wait for this person. Or
let's say you're meeting a friend for lunch, and she's 10
minutes late because of traffic. Suppose you visit your
doctor's office for an appointment only to discover your
doctor is running behind by 20 minutes. Or what if your
car breaks down on your way to work? You call a tow truck
and then must wait half an hour for it to show up.

Such circumstances can transpire despite our best efforts to avoid them. When they do so, we're presented with a choice. We can either make the most of these small pockets of unplanned waiting time or allow the time to slip through our fingers, unused and wasted.

12 Things You Can Do While You Wait

You may be surprised by the many ways you can use unscheduled downtime productively. Following are a few ideas to get your creative juices flowing.

1. Listen to a self-improvement audiobook.
2. Read a chapter in your current book.
3. Write in your journal.
4. Make a doctor or dentist appointment.
5. Create a grocery shopping list.
6. Respond to emails and return phone calls.
7. Review your short-term goals, including your progress to date.
8. Rehearse a presentation or speech you're planning to give.
9. Watch an instructive Youtube video.
10. Send a "thinking of you" text to a friend that you haven't seen in a long time.
11. Break down an upcoming project into small tasks.
12. Brainstorm or research fun activities to do with your kids.

We're just scratching the surface, of course. There are countless ways to put waiting time to use, and the ways you choose to use it should reflect your circumstances, responsibilities, and needs. The important thing is that we acknowledge that unscheduled downtime is inevitable and plan for its use ahead of time.

How to Plan For Unscheduled Downtime

You're undoubtedly aware of circumstances in your daily or weekly routine that expose you to potential downtime. For example, you might stop at your favorite coffee shop each morning on the way to your office. There's a chance you'll get stuck in a long line at the drive-thru window. You can plan for this possibility.

Think about situations you're likely to encounter during your day or week. Do you have a doctor's appointment later in the week? If so, plan for the possibility that your doctor will run late. Do you have to cross commuter train tracks to get to your office? Plan for the likelihood that you'll have to wait for a train. That way, instead of getting frustrated, you can put the time to use.

Also, consider all the things you can do and the tasks you can work on if you experience unscheduled downtime. Create a list of these things so you can quickly remind yourself of them when needed. Keep this list on your phone for easy reference.

Commit yourself to not wasting these tiny blocks of unscheduled waiting time. Pledge to make maximum use of them. Then, whenever you're confronted with unplanned downtime, even if only five minutes, refer to your list of things you can do and take action. This habit will become second nature over time.

∾

EXERCISE #13

∾

FIRST, consider all possible situations that can leave you with unplanned downtime. Write them down.

Some will likely be predictable. Examples include waiting for your dentist, getting caught in rush-hour traffic, and waiting for a coworker to get back to you with needed data. Others will be less predictable. For example, your car might break down. Or you may need to rush a friend to the hospital and wait for them in the waiting room.

Second, create a list of things you can do and items you can work on during this downtime. Use the list above for inspiration. Write these items down or input them into your phone. Whichever option you choose, make sure you have them within reach.

This exercise aims to formalize the process of using your unscheduled downtime. We often let this time slip through our fingers because we lack a systematized method for putting it to productive use.

We've now resolved that oversight. The next time you find yourself waiting around for someone (or something), pull out your list and take action.

Time required: 15 minutes.

TACTIC #14: APPLY PARKINSON'S LAW TO EVERY TASK

∼

One of the most impactful principles regarding time management and productivity that I've seen is Parkinson's law. First expressed in *The Economist* in 1955 by Cyril Northcote Parkinson, it asserts the following:

" Work expands so as to fill the time available for its completion."

I've found this precept to be consistently accurate. If I give myself two hours to audit my quarterly sales data, that job will invariably take me two hours to complete. If I give myself six months to write the first draft of a book, writing that draft will take me six months.

It seems like magic, but it's human nature. Deadlines

motivate us and inspire us to act. This includes deadlines that we impose upon ourselves. To that end, I now apply Parkinson's law to nearly every task and project I undertake. Doing so not only helps me get more done in less time, but I've also found that it helps me better *manage* my time.

When I organize my daily calendar into time blocks (Tactic #1), I decide how much time I'll allow for each task. When I schedule long-term projects on my monthly calendar, I can influence how long these projects will take to complete. The less time I allow myself, the faster I'll finish them (to an extent).

There's a good chance you already use Parkinson's law in your professional and personal life. You may even do so without realizing it. For example, have you ever had to rush to finish grocery shopping because you needed to pick up your kids from school? Ever had to check and respond to emails at breakneck speed because the rest of your day was devoted to meetings?

If so, that was Parkinson's law at work. It forced you to be more efficient because your time was severely limited.

These are examples of how you might have benefitted from Parkinson's law in a random, unplanned fashion. Let's use it *proactively* to utilize our time better. Let's look at how we can take full advantage of Parkinson's law to improve our time management and productivity.

How to Use Parkinson's Law to Your Advantage

The most important prerequisite to using Parkinson's law is accurately estimating how much time a given task should take. For example, suppose you're writing a novel. You must know how long it takes you to write an average chapter. If you're creating a weekly sales spreadsheet for your boss, you must be able to approximate how much time doing so will require.

It's important to review your time estimations, especially in the beginning, to check whether you're giving yourself too much latitude. For instance, you might know from experience that you can write a chapter of your novel in 90 minutes. So don't give yourself two hours to do so. Give yourself 90 minutes. Use that as your baseline.

Your ability to make accurate time estimations will improve the more often you perform a job. Experience is valuable in this regard. If you're about to undertake a new task, you can forecast the amount of time you'll need, but your forecast is likely to be little more than a guess. That's fine. Make your best guess based on available information and resources and adjust later as needed.

Also, include breaks in your forecast. If you know that a task will take you two hours to complete and intend to take three 10-minute breaks during that time, give yourself two and a half hours.

It's easier to apply Parkinson's law when working independently than with others. Making accurate time estimations is more difficult when collaborating with coworkers or waiting for someone to get back to you with needed information.

There's no easy solution to this problem. Experience will help, but the more people involved, the less control you'll have over the process. Make your best guess and take notes. At the very least, you can identify potential bottlenecks (e.g., a lazy or non-responsive coworker) that'll help you improve your time estimations.

3 Quick Tips for Setting Self-Imposed Deadlines

The key here is accuracy. To take full advantage of Parkinson's law, you must be able to make time estimations with some degree of precision. Here are a few tips for doing so.

First, note all of the resources you'll need ahead of time. Do you require specific equipment to complete the task in question? Will you need any support (technical support, subject matter expertise, etc.)? It's important to recognize these needs and ensure you have access to them. Otherwise, you risk wasting time if you're forced to wait for them.

Second, regularly review your time estimations. Optimize them based on your experience. If you've performed a task each week for the past year, you'll be able to predict how much time it'll require accurately. Without that experience, however, your prediction will be partly guesswork. There will undoubtedly be room for improvement. After you've completed the task in question, record how long it took. Note bottlenecks that you encountered along the way. Then make the necessary adjustments.

Third, break down large projects with many moving parts into smaller tasks. Then estimate how much time each task will require. This granularity will improve the accuracy of your time estimations. If you try to estimate how long the entire project will take to complete without first breaking it down, too many unseen variables can undermine your accuracy.

One last note: you must commit to your time estimations to make Parkinson's law work for you. If you estimate that a task will require 30 minutes to complete, commit to stopping after 30 minutes, even if you haven't performed at your highest standard. This will take time to get used to, especially if you entertain perfectionistic tendencies.

~

EXERCISE #14

~

THIS EXERCISE WILL TAKE you through the process of applying Parkinson's law. It's a simple process but worth going through step by step if you've never done it.

First, pick a task or project that you plan to work on. If possible, select one you can do yourself without input from others. For example, you might decide to clean your bathroom for this exercise.

Second, estimate how much time you think you'll need to complete this task or project. If you've performed it in the past, rely on that experience. For instance, you might know that cleaning your bathroom typically takes 45 minutes. Make your best guess if you've never performed the task in question.

Third, perform the task to completion. Record how much time it requires.

Fourth, evaluate the accuracy of your time estimate. Note any bottlenecks or avoidable delays. For example, did you lack cleaning supplies and thus need to buy them? Were you distracted by texts or phone calls?

Lastly, adjust your time estimate for this particular task based on your evaluation. For instance, you might decide that you can clean your bathroom in 30 minutes if you have the needed supplies and work without distraction.

Time required: 10 minutes (excluding performing the task).

TACTIC #15: CATER TO YOUR ENERGY LEVELS

~

Our time management is inextricably entwined with our productivity. The more productive we are, the more control we have over how we use our limited time.

One of the most common oversights in this calculation is the influence of our energy levels. We are most productive when our energy levels are high. And the inverse is true: We are least productive when our energy levels are depleted. We feel mentally, emotionally, and even physically exhausted. We're unable to focus, unmotivated, and uninspired. This state has a measurable effect on our productivity and, by extension, our time management.

We needlessly spin our wheels when we ignore our energy levels and waste precious time. We overlook our productivity zone and fail to take full advantage of it.

But it doesn't have to be this way. We can track how our energy fluctuates throughout the day by taking a few proactive steps and learning to leverage it. The rewards are worth the effort. We'll be more productive and enjoy greater control over our schedules. And we'll experience more latitude to pursue and maintain a healthy work-life balance.

It's a tall order so let's get started.

How to Identify Your Energy Zones

The first thing we need to do is perform an energy audit. This is a quick and easy method for appraising your energy levels and determining their typical fluctuations during a normal day. This audit involves monitoring your levels for a few weeks to note trends and patterns. Once we've identified your natural rhythm and peak energy periods, you'll be able to schedule tasks and projects in a way that fully leverages them.

Before we get started, let's define "energy" for this discussion. I recommend that we do so regarding how motivated, inspired, focused, and productive you feel at any given moment. Admittedly, this is an unscientific approach. After all, how we feel can be influenced by various factors, such as diet, exercise, sleep, and even the status of our interpersonal relationships. But it'll suffice for our purposes.

We'll use a simple numeric scale to gauge your energy levels. I suggest using the numbers 1 through 10, where "1" indicates a dismally low energy level and "10" means that you're nearly bursting with energy (as we've defined it above).

Each hour, evaluate your energy level. Do you feel alert, motivated, and inspired? Are you able to focus? Or do you feel distracted, bored, or apathetic? Rate your level between one and 10.

At the end of your workday, you'll have between 10 and 12 data points (assuming you begin at 8:00 a.m. and track your levels until 7:00 p.m.). Do this each day for three weeks. At the end of three weeks, review your data.

You'll likely recognize patterns. For example, you might notice that your energy levels are consistently rated a "5" from 1:00 p.m. to 2:30 p.m. (following lunch). You may observe that your energy levels are typically between "8" and "9" from 9:00 a.m. to 11:00 a.m.

One quick note: you can do this on a spreadsheet and create a line graph from your data. It looks nice but is overkill, in my opinion. I recommend creating, downloading, and printing a simple daily calendar.[1] Keep it nearby and make your entries on the hour.

How to Take Advantage of Your Peak Zones

You've no doubt heard of the body's circadian rhythm. This is a 24-hour sleep-wake cycle that all of us experience. It influences us mentally and physically and can affect how much energy we have when awake.

But let's dig a little deeper. The body's *ultradian* rhythm is a cycle that repeats throughout the day. Each cycle lasts a couple of hours, during which our energy ebbs and flows. With it, our levels of alertness and performance also do so.

Our goal is to work *with* our body's natural rhythm rather than against it. This means tackling challenging tasks during the high points of our ultradian cycle and working on easy tasks (or taking breaks) during the low points. Doing so helps us to maximize our productivity. We can get more done in less time, giving us more control over how we *use* our time.

You'll see this ultradian rhythm in action by tracking your energy levels throughout the day. It won't look as uniform as the following image (again, numerous factors affect it), but you get the idea:

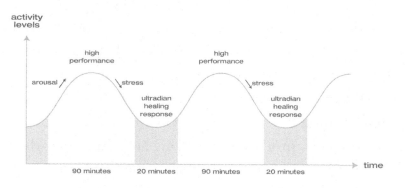

Once you've identified this rhythm and mapped it to your typical workday, you can create a daily schedule that fully leverages it. You'll be able to take full advantage of the bursts of energy you experience throughout the day and give your body and mind the rest they need when they need it.

How to Manage (And Protect) Your Energy

Our energy levels rise and fall like a tide with reasonable predictability. But we can do plenty to preserve them, boosting our "staying power."

As an analogy, consider the many ways we can save fuel while driving. We can refrain from allowing our engine to idle needlessly. We can avoid flooring the pedal. We can keep the engine tuned.

Our energy is like the fuel we put into our vehicles. It is steadily consumed and must be regularly replenished. But like fuel, we can take practical steps to make it last longer.

For example, rebuff energy "vampires." These are people who crave constant attention and emotional support. They often involve needless drama and present themselves as victims in most situations.

We're not talking about friends or loved ones going through difficult, extraordinary circumstances (e.g., divorce, job loss, etc.). Instead, we're talking about the folks who are ceaselessly consumed with their issues and seek to pull everyone around them into their orbit.

Another way to preserve your energy is to set work-related boundaries for yourself. Decide in advance what you're willing and unwilling to do. For example, suppose you're writing a novel. You might decide to restrict your writing time to the morning hours (e.g., 8:00 a.m. to 11:00

a.m.). Or let's say you have a corporate job. You may resolve to refrain from working on the weekends (to the extent that's possible).

You should also give yourself time to recover after periods of deep focus and purposeful activity. Recovery can come in the form of tiny breaks following short time blocks, afternoon catnaps, and occasional vacations. The point is that you allow yourself to rest and refuel.

Lastly, practice healthy habits. This includes eating nutritious foods, regularly exercising, and getting sufficient sleep. Many people place a high value on their productivity and time management but sabotage themselves by neglecting their health. Our physical and mental health impacts our productivity and time management more than you might realize.

∿

EXERCISE #15

∿

THIS SIMPLE EXERCISE highlights your energy levels for a single day. It will encourage you to develop the habit of anticipating them (instead of reacting to them) to build your day around them.

First, print a daily calendar that details the day by the hour (use the resource provided in the endnotes of this chapter). Alternatively, create one using pen and paper.

Next, monitor how you feel each hour, on the hour. For example, at 10:00 a.m., stop what you're doing and gauge your energy level. Are you focused or distracted? Do you feel alert or sleepy? Are you motivated to get things done or having difficulty taking action? Assign a number between 1 and 10 to indicate your energy level. Go through this process at 11:00 a.m., noon, 1:00 p.m., etc., until the end of your workday.

Lastly, review your numbers. Notice when your energy was high. Notice when it was low. Recall what you were working on (or *attempting* to work on) during these time-frames. Is there any way you can adjust your schedule to align it better with these ebbs and flows of your energy levels?

Time required: 15 minutes (combined time of the hourly appraisals).

---

1. Here's a useful, free online resource for creating customized calendars: https://www.timeanddate.com/calendar/create.html?typ=5

TACTIC #16: CREATE (AND STICK TO!) A PRODUCTIVE DAILY ROUTINE

~

Any routine we carry out with purpose improves our time management. Routine reduces the unpredictability of our day. It gives us structure and, therefore, more control over how our day progresses. Routine lessens the degree to which uncertainty influences our behaviors, decisions, and actions. It allows us to schedule each day with a sense of familiarity. Performing the same tasks at the same time each day helps us to stay on track despite the distractions that surround us.

Of course, crises that demand our immediate attention can occur at any time. There's no way to avoid legitimate emergencies. But when we follow a daily routine, we're less likely to be distracted by circumstances that *seem* urgent but aren't so. Our daily routine insulates us, protecting our time, energy, and attentional resources.

This insulation offers crucial mental health benefits. Because we're better able to focus without constantly being at the mercy of distractions, we're less likely to feel stressed, overwhelmed, and burnt out. Our routine prompts us to stick to carefully planned time blocks during which we can work on one thing at a time, single-tasking rather than multitasking. Thus, we can exert significant control over how we spend our limited time and energy and determine which items receive our attention.

How to Create a Productive Daily Routine

There are countless ways to design a daily routine. Your routine should reflect your circumstances, responsibilities, and interests. I'll share the approach that works best for me. It considers several of the time management techniques discussed in previous chapters. I'll highlight them along the way.

First, write down every task and activity that you carry out daily. Here are some examples from which to create your list.

- meals
- breaks
- commute (to and from the workplace)
- read and respond to emails
- listen to and return voicemails
- morning staff meeting
- afternoon sales team meeting

- meet with clients
- review daily sales report
- review online analytics
- write a blog post for the company website
- one-on-one meeting with your boss
- pick up your kids from school

Second, note the tasks and activities that must occur at specific times each day. Write down the corresponding start and estimated stop times next to each item.

For example, you might be required to attend a staff meeting from 9:00 a.m. to 9:30 a.m. each morning. You may need to pick up your kids from school at 3:30 p.m. sharp. Put these items on your daily calendar as time blocks (Tactics #1 and #2). If possible, color them light red to signify that they're inflexible. You have minimal latitude with them and cannot move them around.

Third, prioritize the remaining tasks and activities on your list (Tactic #3). Keep it simple by assigning A, B, or C to each item based on its importance and urgency.

Fourth, identify when your energy levels tend to be high throughout the day and when they tend to wane (Tactic #15). Make a note of these times. We'll come back to them in a moment.

Fifth, determine the amount of focus and creativity each item requires from you. For example, checking and responding to emails will require less focus and creativity than writing a blog post for your company's website. Assign 1, 2, or 3 to each item based on this requisite.

Sixth, review how your energy levels tend to fluctuate and how much focus and creativity each item requires. Schedule time blocks accordingly on your daily calendar. For example, if your energy level is highest from 8:00 a.m to noon, schedule tasks and activities that require significant focus and creativity during this timeframe. Schedule the remaining tasks and activities during the afternoon.

You've now created a productive daily routine. It considers your energy levels, the differing demands of each task and activity, and each item's priority. You can also see which items and their corresponding time blocks cannot be moved or adjusted on your daily calendar.

If you follow the routine you've created, it'll eventually become a habit. As this occurs, you'll be less likely to procrastinate and waste time and more likely to get through your daily to-do list. Assuming you've included time away from work into your routine, you'll also enjoy a better work-life balance.

Of course, creating a daily routine doesn't guarantee you'll stick to it, especially in the beginning. Following your routine until it becomes a force of habit is easier said than done. So let's explore how to act purposefully toward this end.

How to Stick To Your Daily Routine

Making your daily routine a habit is similar to adopting *any* new habit. It will take time and consistent practice. If you stumble along the way, show yourself patience. You will eventually succeed if you remain committed to this goal. Here are a few ideas to help you to streamline, and perhaps even accelerate, the process.

First, be willing to adjust your routine if it doesn't work. Your first daily routine won't be perfect. You might underestimate the time required to complete specific tasks (ref. to Tactic #14). You may find that certain activities are unnecessary or redundant and, therefore, a waste of time. Look for opportunities to optimize your daily routine and align it with your goals, priorities, interests, and energy levels.

Second, use a single online calendar. Down the road, you may find it beneficial to use several calendars, each based on a different context. I do this myself. When you're getting started, however, this is overkill and likely to get in the way of developing the daily routine habit. Put your schedule in one place, including all of your time blocks.

Third, sticking to your daily routine will be easier if you can concentrate. Your routine will be composed of individual time blocks, each assigned to a specific task or activity. When you do the job or activity in question at the specified time, free of distraction, you train your brain to adopt that particular pattern.

For example, I write at the same time every morning. I've been doing so for a long time. My brain expects to be in "writing mode" at that time, which has helped make the habit stick.

Fourth, make sure you include breaks on your calendar. It may seem strange to block off time for 5-minute and 10-

minute breaks, but if you neglect to do so, there's a good chance you won't take them. Your brain needs to learn *when* to take breaks like it needs to know when to perform other tasks and activities.

Your daily routine will continuously remind you what you should be doing and when you should be doing it. Once it becomes a force of habit, you'll discover that it increases your efficiency and productivity. If you get distracted, your routine will help you to get back on track quickly.

~

EXERCISE #16

~

IN THIS EXERCISE, we'll create a simple routine that covers the first half of your day.

First, write down every task and activity you need or want to accomplish between 8:00 a.m. and noon. This might include working out, writing in a journal, or responding to emails. It may involve eating breakfast, dropping your kids off at school, or perusing the latest financial news. Write all of it down.

Second, note which items must be done at specific times. An example is dropping your kids off at school. Assign a time block for this item on your calendar and color code it red. Red means it cannot be moved or abandoned.

Third, assign priorities to your remaining items. Use A, B, and C to signify priority levels.

Fourth, if your energy fluctuates between 8:00 a.m. and noon, note when it is highest and when it is lowest. Be as specific as possible.

Fifth, ascertain how much focus and creativity each item will require. Use 1, 2, and 3 to indicate this demand.

Sixth, schedule each item according to your priorities, energy levels, and how much focus and creativity they require. Assign time blocks for each one.

The purpose of this exercise is to formalize your daily routine. Doing so lets you quickly note where your routine can be improved or adjusted to suit your needs.

Time required: 15 minutes.

TACTIC #17: IMPROVE YOUR WORKING MEMORY

~

Have you ever made a mental grocery list and visited the grocery store only to have forgotten what you had intended to buy? Ever misplaced your keys and had difficulty finding them? Ever needed a friend or colleague to provide information that they have given you multiple times that day? If so, you've experienced an imperfect working memory.

Working memory refers to our cognitive ability to retain information and use it to make decisions temporarily, reason through arguments, and perform other mental tasks. It's often confused with short-term memory, but it is slightly different.[1]

We rely on working memory and use it in countless ways during a typical day. We also regularly suffer consequences associated with poor working memory. For example, have you ever forgotten a person's name, read a paragraph repeatedly for comprehension, or had trouble remembering what you wanted to say during a conversation?

When our working memory is weak, we are prone to make avoidable mistakes and waste time compensating for them. The good news is that we can improve our working memory. As we do so, we naturally improve our productivity, time management, and overall performance in our personal and professional lives.

The Connection between Working Memory and Time Management

Whenever we start working on a task, our brain refers to all the information and instructions it has in short-term storage about that task. If its retention is good, you can get to work quickly and efficiently. If its retention is poor, you'll need time to review the requisite details before you start working.[2]

A strong working memory accelerates and enhances our cognitive function. We're able to process and make use of information more quickly and effectively. We can make faster decisions that align with our intentions and goals. We're more capable of crafting workarounds in response to obstacles. We can achieve deeper focus and avoid being sidetracked by distractions and disruptions.

In this state, we're more productive. We have a firmer grasp of which tasks and projects are most important and are inclined to prioritize them accordingly. We're better able to coordinate our decisions, actions, and responses based on the information we can retrieve from short-term storage. As such, we're more prepared to take immediate, purposeful action rather than procrastinating due to doubt and uncertainty.

How to Improve Your Working Memory

Until as recently as the 1990s, it was widely believed that working memory couldn't be improved, at least not by any noticeable measure. Recent research, however, suggests that this conclusion was incorrect.[3] Additional research conducted in the field of ADHD has demonstrated similar findings.[4]

Assuming that we can proactively improve our working memory, how should we go about doing so? Following are several things you can do starting today to bolster this crucial piece of your executive functioning skills. Note that a few align with tactics we've covered in previous chapters (and one we'll cover in the following chapter). If you're already doing them, you're ahead of the game.

First, break down large chunks of information into smaller portions whenever possible. For example, consider how phone numbers are formatted. Phone numbers would be far more difficult to remember without hyphens to break up the string of digits. But breaking the string into smaller pieces eases the burden and streamlines recall.

Second, follow routines. The more you rely on patterns

and procedures, the less your brain will need to retrieve the stored information. For example, if you put your keys in the same place every time you arrive home, your brain won't need to recall where you left them. This frees up your working memory for other details.

Third, don't multitask. Research suggests that multi-taskers tend to underperform single-taskers when doing activities that require working memory.[5] The former tend to experience bouts of forgetfulness and lapses in alertness.[6]

Fourth, do simple exercises designed to challenge your working memory. For example, write down ten nouns. Now, without looking at the list, recall the first two. Then try to remember the first three. Then, four and so on until you can recall the entire list (in order).

Fifth, use to-do lists and checklists. The more you can rely on these tools, the less information your brain will need to retrieve from working memory (similar to following routines). This leaves more capacity for other details.

Sixth, play card games. Poker, gin rummy, and similar games encourage you to remember the cards you've seen (in addition to the rules). If you're alone, pick ten random cards from a standard deck. Note the numbers (or values for face cards) and suits. Then try to recall the cards in the order you selected them.

~

EXERCISE #17

THIS EXERCISE WILL REVEAL whether there's room to improve your working memory.[7] We'll use a scale from 1 to 10 to indicate how often each of the below incidents occurs. One means that it seldom happens, and ten means it frequently happens.

Think back to conversations you've had with friends, coworkers, colleagues, and family members. Did you have difficulty following the discussions? Does this seldom happen or frequently happen? Assign an appropriate value between 1 and 10.

Recall times you've lost track of personal items, such as your glasses, keys, and phone. Seldom or frequent? Assign a value between 1 and 10.

Think of times when you've forgotten important steps in multistep projects. An example is preparing a complicated meal and forgetting a key ingredient. Another example is planning to host a party and forgetting to buy ice for drinks. Assign a value between 1 and 10.

Consider when you've forgotten people's names despite having recently met them. Assign a value between 1 and 10.

Now, let's review our numbers. If you've assigned a value higher than 5 in any of the above departments, there's room to improve your working memory.

Time required: 20 minutes.

1. Short-term memory refers to our ability to retain information for a very short period, shorter than is possible with working memory.
2. The cache of your web browser works similarly. Pieces of information are stored temporarily when you visit websites. These pieces include bits of HTML, javascript, and images. When you return to these sites, your browser refers to its cache. It can load the sites more quickly than would be possible if it didn't possess these pieces.
3. Bopp, Kara L. and Verhaeghen, Paul (2010, December) Working Memory and Aging: Separating the Effects of Content and Context. *Psychological Aging*, 24(4), pages 968–980, https://doi.org/10.1037%2Fa0017731
4. Klingberg, T., et. al. (2005, February 1) Computerized training of working memory in children with ADHD--a randomized, controlled trial. *Journal of the American Academy of Child and Adolescent Psychiatry*, 44(2), pages 177-186, https://doi.org/10.1097/00004583-200502000-00010
5. Uncapher, Melina R. and Anthony, Wager D. (2018, October 1) Minds and brains of media multitaskers: Current findings and future directions. *PNAS*, 115(40), pages 9889-9896, https://doi.org/10.1073/pnas.1611612115
6. Madore, Kevin P., et. al. (2020, October 28) Memory failure predicted by attention lapsing and media multitasking. Nature, 587(7832), pages 87-91, https://doi.org/10.1038/s41586-020-2870-z
7. Most people, including yours truly, have room for improvement in this area.

TACTIC #18: BECOME A TO-DO LIST MASTER

~

To-do lists increase our productivity while helping us to avoid feeling overwhelmed in the process. They provide a valuable bird's-eye view of what we hope to accomplish daily.

To-do lists also mitigate the mental strain we experience throughout the day. When we feel unfocused, we can lean on their structure and organization. When we feel unmotivated or uninspired, we can look at our to-do list and recover a sense of ownership and accountability. When we feel stressed by the demands on our time and attentional resources, our to-do list gives us a sense of order, alleviating the pressure.

Writing down tasks helps us prioritize the most important ones and allocate our time accordingly. To this end alone, to-do lists are an indispensable time management tool. Whether you're a corporate manager, student, freelancer, or stay-at-home parent, they're invaluable.

Unfortunately, many people who regularly create daily to-do lists make mistakes that hamper their effectiveness. These mistakes can be easily avoided, but we must first identify them.

The 4 Most Common To-Do List Mistakes

One of the most frequent blunders I've seen when creating to-do lists is to make them too long. Earlier in this book, we discussed confusing busyness for productivity (ref. Mistake #6). This confusion is demonstrated in excessively long to-do lists.[1]

The ideal daily to-do list will contain no more than ten tasks. (I prefer to limit my daily lists to five.) This constraint will keep you focused and encourage you to prioritize tasks and allot your time between the most important ones.

A second common mistake is neglecting to estimate how much time each task will require. A list of tasks has limited value on its own. We need to know how long each one will take to complete to assign them to accurate time blocks.

This leads us to a third mistake: failing to use a daily calendar jointly with a daily to-do list. By themselves, to-do lists lack intentionality. They show a list of things to do but offer no insight regarding when to do them and how long to spend on them. Consequently, items are left unaddressed and repeatedly moved forward to the following day.

Fourth, many people create their to-do lists on the morning of the day they intend to use their lists. This practice encourages them to rush the process. In doing so, they risk overlooking important tasks and failing to prioritize the ones they add. They also risk neglecting to estimate times to completion.

Again, these mistakes can be easily avoided. It's mostly a matter of sticking to a few best practices.

12 Quick Tips for Creating To-Do Lists That Work

There's no single perfect to-do list system. What works best for you will differ from what works best for someone else. So it's worthwhile to test everything. Keep what suits you and jettison the rest.

Here are 12 best practices that will make your daily to-do lists more effective and improve your overall task management system.

1. Capture everything on a "brain dump" list. Transfer items from this list to your daily to-do lists according to priority and workflow.
2. Determine whether a single task is too inclusive and should be broken down into smaller, more manageable tasks.
3. Prioritize each task. Use a simple A through E, or 1 through 5, system. Keep in mind that "urgent" doesn't always mean "important" (Tactic #3).

4. Estimate the amount of time each task will take to complete.

5. Place tasks from your to-do list onto a daily calendar (Tactic #2). Use time blocks (Tactic #1) based on your estimates to completion.

6. Batch similar tasks together and address them during the same time block (Tactic #12).

7. Limit your daily to-do lists to 10 items (and preferably five).

8. Avoid placing goals on your to-do list. "Learn to speak French" is not an appropriate to-do item. "Learn five new French adjectives" is better.

9. Assign one task as your "MIT" (most important task). This task must be completed, even if nothing else gets done.

10. Create your daily to-do lists the night before. Take the time you need to prioritize items and schedule them on your daily calendar according to how your energy levels fluctuate (Tactic #15).

11. Use Parkinson's law when assigning to-do items to time blocks on your daily calendar. This will counter and discourage perfectionism (Tactic #14).

12. Review your performance at the end of each day. Did you complete every task on your daily to-do list? If not, determine the reason. For example, your list might have included too many items. Or one of the items may have

been too large and should have been broken down into smaller tasks.

Your daily to-do lists should help you to complete your most important tasks and projects. But if you create them using the wrong approach, they'll be just as likely to make you feel ineffectual. I recommend using the 12 best practices above. At least test them. If you find that one or more fail to work for you — or worse, impede your workflow and time management — disregard them.

~

EXERCISE #18

~

IN THIS EXERCISE, we'll create a simple, barebones to-do list system.[2] It will hark back to a few tactics we've previously discussed and address several of the best practices noted above.

First, create a "brain dump" list. Brainstorm everything you'd like to accomplish and everything that will require your time and attention. This might require significant time. Don't feel that you must complete this step before moving on. You'll almost certainly think of items to add to this list later.

Second, prioritize every item on your "brain dump" list. Assign each item a value between 1 and 5. The highest-priority items receive a "1," and the lowest-priority items receive a "5."

Third, estimate how much time each item on your "brain dump" list will require to complete.

Fourth, transfer five tasks from your "brain dump" list to your next daily to-do list. These items should align with your priorities and available time.

Fifth, assign one of the five transferred tasks as your MIT.

Sixth, place the five transferred tasks on your daily calendar. Assign time blocks based on each task's estimated time to completion and Parkinson's law. (Don't forget to add breaks to your calendar.)

Seventh, review your performance at the end of the day. Identify the reason you couldn't complete every item on your to-do list.

Time required: 30 minutes.

---

1. There is a place for large to-do lists. These are "brain dump" lists. Daily to-do lists should be kept short.
2. My book *To-Do List Formula* details a far more comprehensive system.

TACTIC #19: ATTEND (AND SCHEDULE) FEWER MEETINGS

~

eetings *can* be useful in select circumstances. They allow participants to share ideas. They offer a platform for collaboration and team building. They can encourage creativity and accelerate decision-making. And they can even improve or reinforce a sense of connection with colleagues.

On paper, meetings seem highly beneficial. In reality, they're usually a waste of time. And when you're already struggling to find time in your schedule to manage your workload, being trapped in unnecessary meetings can be a frustrating, miserable experience.

Why are most meetings a waste of time? First, they're too long. Even when they finish within the allotted time, they rarely justify occupying that time. How often have you been trapped in an hour-long meeting that could've been completed in 15 minutes?

Second, they're often unfocused. Attendees discuss irrelevant matters because the leader of the meeting fails to keep them on point.

Third, they often start late. Attendees arrive late, presuming others will wait for them. If it's a recurring meeting, this expectation grows with time. Before long, everyone begins to arrive after the meeting's established start time, putting everyone behind schedule.

Fourth, meetings are often completely unnecessary. Salient information can be delivered and discussed more efficiently via email, phone, or in person one-on-one.

Making matters worse, meetings give the mistaken impression of progress. Attendees feel they're making headway on projects simply because they attended a meeting. This is usually a mirage.

The fewer meetings you attend, the more time you'll have at your disposal to work on tasks and projects that are important to you. So let's explore a few ways to avoid unnecessary meetings without severe consequences.

How to Avoid Unnecessary Meetings

I'll start by conceding that the following tips may or may not be feasible depending on your circumstances. You might not be able to control which meetings you attend and avoid. If that's the case, I can empathize with your predicament. I endured a similar experience when I had a corporate job and know it's common.

You may have more control than you realize, however. (This, too, was my experience in my corporate job.) So I encourage you to try the following tips and note your results. You might discover that you can steer clear of some meetings that you had previously thought were inescapable.

First, decline the meeting invitation. It's common for meeting organizers to invite people who don't need to attend. Often they do so out of courtesy. If your presence at a meeting is unnecessary, opt out of it. You might be able to do so by simply not showing up (other attendees may assume you're busy with more important matters). Otherwise, send a short note to the organizer politely declining the invitation. If the organizer feels your presence is crucial, they will let you know.

Second, put time blocks on your calendar so everyone can see them. Organizers often choose their meetings' dates and times based on others' availability. Blocking off time can help you to avoid these meetings. If your presence is necessary, the organizer will try to accommodate your schedule.

Third, if someone proposes an in-person meeting, counter-propose a phone call. Meetings often last longer than necessary because participants lounge together in a relaxed environment away from their duties and projects. A simple phone call may suffice and will almost surely consume less time.

Fourth, if you must attend a meeting, let the organizer know you have less time available than the proposed duration. For example, if the organizer proposes an hour-long meeting, tell them, *"I only have 30 minutes available during that time slot. When would you suggest I arrive to make the best use of that 30 minutes?"*

One last note: many people try to reduce the number of meetings they attend by proposing a "no meeting" day each week. This tactic rarely works. Instead, unnecessary meetings are postponed and rescheduled. A better approach is to master the art of declining meetings, including saying no to invitations and suggesting alternatives and workarounds.

How to Run Efficient Meetings

Let's switch gears. Rather than receiving (and desperately trying to decline) invitations to meetings, you're now the one proposing them. Assuming these meetings are necessary, the question is, "how can you run them as efficiently as possible, saving everyone time in the process?" Here are a few best practices to ensure your meetings are as productive as possible.

First, have a clear purpose and plan regarding what you'd like to cover during the meeting. Arrive with a detailed, focused agenda. Send it to attendees beforehand, so they'll (hopefully) arrive with it, too.

Second, ask attendees to turn their phones off. Fair warning: you may run into resistance. But if you encourage attendees to comply, you'll face fewer interruptions and distractions.

Third, set an aggressive meeting duration. The most common meeting length is an hour. But not all meetings need that amount of time. Think of Parkinson's law (Tactic #14). If you allot an hour, there's a good chance your meeting will fill the entire hour. Try 45 minutes. Try 35 minutes. You'll find that setting a shorter duration will encourage everyone to focus.

Fourth, ask attendees to hold off on discussing topics not listed in your agenda. Squelch side discussions before they gain momentum.

Fifth, set aside five minutes at the end of the meeting to detail an action plan. Ask attendees to be responsible for specific deliverables and their accompanying deadlines. Plan these; they'll comprise your meeting agenda's "hidden" part.

Finally, ask yourself whether a meeting is truly necessary. Are you proposing it just because you believe you should? Or do you have a clear purpose? Is meeting in person vital, or would email suffice? One of the best ways to steer clear of an inefficient, time-wasting meeting is not to have a meeting.

∼

EXERCISE #19

∼

THIS EXERCISE WILL ENCOURAGE you to review your meeting invitations with a critical eye.

First, write down every meeting you've been asked to attend this week.

Second, describe each meeting's objective. Summarize it as concisely as possible. If the organizer hasn't provided the purpose, ask them for clarification.

Third, write down each meeting's proposed duration.

Fourth, ask yourself whether you'll have anything significant to present for each meeting. Will you be expected to provide pivotal data or ideas? Is your presence necessary, or have you been invited as a courtesy?

Lastly, highlight the meetings that are likely to waste your time. Note how much time you'll save if you decline the invitations. If being a no-show isn't an option, reach out to the organizer to formally decline.

Time required: 15 minutes.

TACTIC #20: DEVELOP SMART ORGANIZATIONAL SKILLS

~

Organizational skills are the unsung hero of productivity and time management. Most people acknowledge their importance. But the advice to "get organized" is so conventional (even clichéd) that it's often overlooked or instinctively disregarded.

The problem is that many people work and live in a state of chronic disorganization despite recognizing that doing so impedes their productivity and time management. They get used to clutter. They become accustomed to losing track of important items and vital information and looking for them, often desperately, as deadlines loom.

If you struggle with this issue, I have good news: it can be corrected easily by taking a few practical steps. Like any skill, you can learn to be organized. It just takes a bit of time and the willingness to reverse a self-sabotaging pattern.

Below we'll review several organizational best practices that will help you to manage your time. Some will do so without requiring any effort on your part. Once you develop these skills and make them habits, they'll pay dividends without calling attention to themselves.

The upside? You'll find yourself doing better quality work, making fewer mistakes, and completing tasks and projects on time. Without clutter holding you hostage, you'll work more efficiently, experience less stress, and enjoy a better work-life balance. You might even sleep better.

Big promises, I know. But if you're practicing good organizational skills for the first time, don't be surprised if doing so improves your quality of life.

5 Areas to Apply Good Organizational Skills

The first area that deserves attention is your workspace. Once a tiny bit of clutter is allowed to persist unchecked, it can quickly snowball to take over your desk, cubicle, or home office. Here are a few quick tips to prevent this from happening:

- Limit the number of office supplies on your desk. Keep one or two pens, a small paper pad, and a stapler. Put everything else in a drawer.

- Keep your phone and other gadgets out of sight. They'll be less distracting in a drawer or a different room if you work at home.
- Throw items away the moment you decide they belong in the trash. Don't allow them to pile up.

A second area is your filing system. A sound system will make it easier to find things when you need to retrieve them. You'll know exactly where they are, saving you time. Here are a few best practices to help you to optimize your filing system:

- Invest in folders and a filing cabinet if you must keep physical files.
- Organize files according to how you would like to look for them. For example, if you're a freelancer, you might organize files by clients' last names. If you're a manager, you may prefer to organize them by deadlines or priority.
- If you keep records on your computer or in the cloud, create an organizational hierarchy that makes sense to you. Nest folders within folders instead of maintaining an endless list of top-level folders.
- Discard files that you no longer need. Shred them if they contain sensitive information. Or delete them if they're on your computer or in the cloud.

The third area to focus on is your note-taking system. If you take a lot of notes, you'll need a method for organizing them. Here are a few suggestions:

- Select a note-taking method and stick with it. The more consistent your notes' structure, the easier it will be to retrieve details later. Use the charting method, the Cornell method, the mapping method, or whatever technique feels most intuitive.
- If you need to organize physical notes, use 3-ring binders or colored notebooks. For example, a red notebook might indicate meeting notes. Green might signify a particular project you're working on. Any visual cue can suffice, but I find colors the best method.
- If you need to organize digital notes, use an app designed for this function. Examples include Evernote, OneNote, and Google Keep. Good apps will allow you to search for notes and create folders for them. So use appropriate keywords that you can search for later.

The fourth area to organize is your prioritization. There are many approaches. I recommend testing several to find which of them best suits you. Don't be afraid to cherrypick elements of various methods to create a tailored system for yourself. Here are a few quick tips (they'll be familiar from previous chapters of this book):

- Adopt a simple prioritization system. For example, assign each task a number between 1 and 5. This will make it easier to organize items according to which ones most deserve your time and immediate attention.
- Color code your top-priority tasks. This is easily done whether you're maintaining physical or digital to-do lists. If you're maintaining physical to-do lists, use a red pen to mark these tasks. If you're maintaining digital to-do lists, use an app with a color coding feature. (I use Todoist, but other good options include Any.do, TickTick, and Google Tasks.
- Review your task list and each item's priority level at least once a week and more often if needed. Priorities can change due to modified goals, availability of resources, and shifting deadlines. Review your list and update the priority levels you had previously assigned to tasks accordingly.

The fifth and final area that warrants maintaining good organizational habits is communication. It's beneficial to stay on top of the information you communicate, the people with whom you share it, and the mode of communication you use. Likewise, it's helpful to organize the information you receive, the people from whom you receive it, and the method of communication they use to deliver it.

Otherwise, tasks and details can fall through the cracks. Here are a few simple tips:

- Keep good notes. Whenever you deliver or receive information, note the date, time, and whether it was in person, by email, or by phone.
- Develop a consistent system. For example, if you're responsible for emailing your boss once a week with an update on a specific project, do so on the same day at the same time (e.g., Tuesday at 10:00 a.m.).
- Use an email program that allows you to tag each email. This will enable you to organize your emails by topic, project, deliverable, and sender or recipient.

Good organizational skills take time to develop and implement with consistency. That's the case whenever you adopt a new habit. But once you do so, you'll save significant time and insulate yourself from the chaos of a hectic day.

How to Get (And Stay!) Organized

It begins with your goals. Your priorities stem from your goals, and you can only get organized once you've identified your priorities. If you haven't yet established your goals, that's where you should start. They should pertain to both your personal and professional lives. They might include your education, career, relationships, and investments.

Once you've set your goals and established your priorities, getting organized becomes a matter of adopting and maintaining the proper habits.

For example, get into the custom of making lists. For example, create a list for each project you oversee, detailing every step that needs to be completed. Create a list for each personal goal you set for yourself, outlining every action you must take to accomplish the goal. You can't expect to remember everything. Put the details on a list so you can retrieve them as needed.

Periodically declutter your workspace. Do this on a schedule (e.g., each Friday afternoon) so that it becomes a part of your routine. You may be surprised at how quickly clutter can accumulate if left untamed.

Speaking of routines (Tactic #16), they're a useful organizational tool. The more you can systematize your day, the greater certainty you'll have that the right to-do items are being addressed. After all, you'll be doing the same things at the same time each day. There's little chance they'll be overlooked.

Take advantage of tools that support your organizational skills and habits whenever possible. For example, an online calendar is preferable to a physical calendar if you need others to access your schedule remotely. If you're a project manager, you'll want to use project management software that supports time tracking, streamlines communication, and encourages collaboration amongst project members. If you're a novelist, you'll need tools to help you organize your novel's settings, beats, tropes, and character details.

Armed with the right tools and habits, you can easily organize every area of your life. Once you do so, you'll find it much easier to manage your time while getting the essential things done.

EXERCISE #20

For this exercise, we'll examine the five areas we discussed earlier. Our goal is to identify opportunities to improve our organizational skills. I encourage you to do this the old-fashioned way. Use pen and paper, jotting down ideas as they come to you. I find it promotes creativity and helps with brainstorming.

Let's move forward in the order we used earlier. First up is your workspace. Observe the surface. Look at the small spaces between the large items, such as your monitor and keyboard. Inspect the periphery. Is there clutter present? Do you notice office supplies that you rarely use, if ever? Are there a lot of personal items, such as vacation photos, knickknacks, and miscellaneous keepsakes? Make a note of these things.

Next up is your filing system. Does it follow a sensible structure or methodology? Is it intuitive? Can you easily find things when you need to do so? If not, what changes could you implement to improve your organization? Write them down.

Let's consider your note-taking. First, what method do you use to take notes? Do you consistently use this method, or do you use whatever way that comes to mind at the time? How do you organize your notes after you take them? Do you follow a particular system? Does this system make finding and retrieving specific notes easier or more difficult? Jot down your thoughts.

Next, reflect on your system of prioritization. How do you currently distinguish between high-priority and low-priority tasks and projects? Do you have a method to highlight the former so they won't be overlooked? How do you ensure that every item on your plate goes through your prioritization system and is formally assigned a priority level? Do you implement this system methodically or haphazardly? Make notes.

Last up is your communication. How do you usually communicate with people during the week? Email? Phone? In-person meetings? Do you have a procedure to record the date, time, and people involved with every communication in which important information is received or delivered? Can you easily retrieve these details? If not, what changes can you make to streamline retrieval? Write them down.

The purpose of this exercise is to perform a comprehensive audit of your organizational habits in these five crucial areas. It allows you to expose oversights and patterns holding you back and make changes to remedy them.

Time required: 30 minutes.

TACTIC #21: USE TECHNOLOGY TO IMPROVE YOUR WORKFLOW

~

Twenty years ago, we relied on pen and paper to manage our time. We created our to-do lists on paper. We outlined our schedules on paper. We tracked our time on paper. We used day planners, desk calendars, and physical tickler files. Those were the tools we had at our disposal, and we made the most of them.

Things are much different today, of course. Most of us rely on software to help us manage our time. Countless apps are available to do the heavy lifting regarding time tracking, project management, task management, and communication. Online calendars have replaced paper-based calendars. To-do list apps have replaced pads of paper.

Life has become increasingly hectic and chaotic. Time management software helps us to keep our heads above water. They support our efforts to create routines, develop good habits, and increase productivity. They facilitate our trying to allocate our time as judiciously as possible given its many demands. Apps allow us to "work smarter, not harder" (although we seem to be working as hard as ever these days).

But not all time management tools are created equal. Some are better than others. And among that smaller group, some will be better suited to you than others. In the following section, we'll examine a few that stand apart from the pack.

7 Time Management Tools I Recommend

Before we start, let me explain how I chose the tools listed below. To make this list, an app needed to be easy to use and receive ongoing support from its developers. The app didn't need to be free (although many of them are). Nor was it necessary for the app to offer a mile-long feature list; I'm only interested in *useful* features.

It (hopefully) goes without saying that none of the developers paid for placement here. I use most of these tools myself.

With that out of the way, let's get started. Here are seven time management tools that outshine the competition.

1. **Todoist**[1] - I've used Todoist to manage my to-do lists for many years. It's available on every

platform, including iOS, Android, and the web. Other to-do list apps offer more features, but Todoist has everything I need. It's flexible without being overly complicated. (Price: free and paid versions available)

2. **Google Calendar**[2] - Like Todoist, I've used this one for years. It offers a surprisingly extensive list of features available for iOS, Android, and the web. You can customize the view, share your calendar with others, and integrate it with other tools, such as Slack, Salesforce, and Zoom. For me, Google Calendar's best feature is its simple interface. (Price: free)

3. **Evernote**[3] - I can't say enough good things about Evernote. It's perfect for taking notes on your phone (Android or iOS), tablet, or via your browser. And it allows you to organize your notes to sort, highlight, and retrieve them quickly. Evernote offers many features I have yet to use and integrates with other tools, including Google Calendar. (Price: free and paid versions available)

4. **Marinara Timer**[4] - You need a timer that alerts you when your time blocks expire. This is the tool I use. Marinara Timer doesn't look like much at first glance (in fact, it looks dated). But it does precisely what it's supposed to do. This tool is only available on the web, so if you're

using it on your phone, you'll need to do so in your phone's browser. (Price: free)

5. **Toggl**[5] - This is the perfect tool for conducting time audits that reveal where you're "leaking" time (Tactic #5). It's available on every major platform, including Windows, macOS, iOS, Android, the web, and even Linux. One of its best features is that there's no setup required. One click, and you're tracking your time. (Price: free and paid versions available)

6. **RescueTime**[6] - This is a productivity tracker. If you let it run in the background, it'll produce detailed reports that reveal the websites on which you spend your time. There's no need to run it every day. Instead, run it whenever you feel like your discipline is slipping and online distractions are hampering you.

7. **Freedom**[7] - If you're finding it difficult to focus, this one might be the answer. Freedom is a website and app-blocking tool. If certain websites (e.g., Reddit, CNN, etc.) or apps (e.g., Instagram, Facebook, etc.) distract you, add them to a block list. You can set a start and end time during which you won't be able to access the sites and apps on your blocklist. And you can create multiple blocklists and edit them whenever you want. It's available on every major platform. (Price: try it for free. If you like it, choose from among the three paid versions.)

Honorable mention: **Trello**[8] - This is a workflow, task management, and project management tool. I don't currently use it because I've found other tools that better suit my particular needs. But I've used it in the past when I wanted to collaborate with others. Trello provides a visual dashboard on which you manage tasks via "cards." You can organize these cards by moving them around on your dashboard and dragging and dropping them as needed. You can share files and images and organize tasks by priority, date, and the individuals to whom they're assigned. It's a powerful tool. (Price: free and paid versions available)

Don't feel you have to use the time management apps highlighted above. If you find others you love, and they're not included in the above list, I encourage you to use them. The most important thing is that you use tools that suit you.

I recommend that you test the seven tools above for yourself. Put each one through its paces. See if they do what you need them to do. And don't be afraid to disregard them if you find better alternatives.

Proceed with Caution

One last note regarding time management tools. The last decade has ushered in a flood of apps and other software designed to help us track and manage our time, organize our workflow, and boost productivity. This is both good and bad.

On the positive side, many of these new tools are helpful. They offer features that have been developed to bridge the gap between what we need and what was previously available.

But there are also potential downsides. First, there's a temptation to use tools for no identified need. This can sometimes lead to using several with overlapping features. I've talked to people who use two or three to-do list apps. Why do they do so? I don't know, and they couldn't explain it.

Second, there's a temptation to jump from the app you're currently using to the newest alternative. This is shiny object syndrome (SOS), and fear of missing out (FOMO) wrapped up in one package.

Here's the bottom line: use whatever tool works for you. Pick one for its purpose (e.g., note-taking, time tracking, etc.) and stick with it. Abandon it only if it no longer meets your needs.

~

EXERCISE #21

~

FOR THIS FINAL EXERCISE, we'll quickly audit your time management tools. The results will reveal whether you're using multiple tools that perform the same functions and encourage you to justify doing so. This audit will also reveal gaps. If you have an identified need (e.g., an online calendar), but you're not currently using an appropriate tool, we'll see that as well.

First, using pen and paper, create the following seven headings:

1. to-do lists
2. calendar
3. note-taking
4. time blocking
5. time tracking
6. productivity
7. distractions

Second, starting with to-do lists, write down the tools you currently use for each purpose. If you're using pen and paper, note that detail. If you're using an app or web-based tool, write down its name.

Third, check whether you use more than one tool to fulfill a category's purpose. An example would be using Evernote and OneNote to take and organize notes. These tools overlap. If you find such overlap, choose one tool in that category and abandon the others.

Fourth, check whether there are any categories for which you're not currently using an app or other tool. For example, you may not now be tracking your time or creating to-do lists. If that's the case, plan to test at least one app that performs this function.

The goal is to choose and use one time management tool for each of the seven purposes listed above. Again, use whatever tool works for you, including pen and paper.

Time required: 15 minutes.

---

1. https://todoist.com/
2. https://www.google.com/calendar/
3. https://evernote.com/
4. https://www.marinaratimer.com/
5. https://toggl.com/track/
6. https://www.rescuetime.com/
7. https://freedom.to/
8. https://trello.com/en

PART IV

HOW TO MANAGE YOUR TIME WHEN LIFE THROWS YOU CURVE BALLS

∼

Unexpected circumstances can wreck our day despite our best intentions and plans. Emergencies can sabotage our calendar. Crises of every type can rear their head anytime, and often just when things are going smoothly for us. When they do so, they can disrupt our focus, ruin our productivity, and wreak havoc with our carefully prepared schedules.

Properly managing our time requires us to be proactive. We try to plan our day ahead of time. But life sometimes forces us into reaction mode. We have no choice but to adapt to random events that negatively affect our plans.

This short section will share a few practical tips on how

to deal with life's curveballs. We can't stop them, and coping with them isn't enough. Instead, we want to minimize their long-term impact so we can manage our time effectively despite circumstances beyond our control.

THE IMPORTANCE OF ADAPTABILITY

∼

Adaptability doesn't receive the attention it deserves. Most of the advice regarding time management is focused on planning. Make good plans, and everything else will fall into place.

But you know from firsthand experience that life isn't so simple. To quote the Scottish poet Robert Burns, "The best laid plans of mice and men often go awry." That's the reason adaptability is so important. It's an essential component of any effective time management strategy.

No organizational tip, efficiency hack, or productivity app will completely insulate you from life's curveballs. It's akin to owning the best cookware money can buy but discover that your main ingredient has turned. Your only option is to adapt. Here are a few suggestions to help you flourish when life goes sideways.

Plan Ahead for Catastrophes

They're going to happen, so we should plan for them. Although we'll never be able to predict how emergencies will present, we *can* outline how we'll respond to them.

For example, suppose a family member has a medical emergency, and you must take them to the hospital. There's no way to anticipate this situation. But you *can* plan how to spend your time in the hospital's waiting room. What files and tools should you take with you? Who must you call to ensure specific projects move ahead in your absence?

It's difficult to focus when emergencies arise. The more we can plan our responses ahead of time, the less we'll need to think them through in the moment of crisis.

Add Buffer Time to Your Schedule

Most circumstances that disrupt our day won't rise to the level of catastrophe. We're far more likely to encounter less extreme situations. For example, you might get a flat tire on your way to work. Your internet connection may suffer an unplanned outage. You might receive a call from your child's school asking you to pick them up following an altercation with another student.

These interruptions could have dire consequences if your calendar is filled with back-to-back time blocks. But if you leave yourself a margin, they'll have a less severe effect.

We discussed buffer time at length in Tactic #2, so we'll not dwell on it here.

Manage Your Emotional Response

When unanticipated situations threaten to demolish our carefully planned schedules, it's natural to respond emotionally. It's good to vent your frustration. Let it out. But avoid dwelling on it. Don't brood over life's unfairness. That leads to more anger.

Once you've acknowledged your distress and aggravation, take a moment to regroup. Think about your next step in light of your options. Then take that step. Taking purposeful action will help you to break free of the emotional quagmire.

Consider the Upside

Look for the silver lining in every cloud. Doing so won't resolve a bad situation, but it can help to minimize its emotional impact.

For example, suppose your child's school suddenly calls and asks you to pick them up. You might think, "Well, I need to get gas and visit the grocery store today. I might as well do that while I'm out."

Or imagine that you're on your way to work and your vehicle gets a flat tire. You're stuck waiting for a tow truck. It's a terrible circumstance, but you might reflect, "Well, at least I don't have to attend the morning sales call."

Sometimes, recognizing a silver lining (even a tiny one) can liberate us from our initial emotional reaction.

Learn to Be Flexible

It sounds like banal advice, and in a way, it is. But it's also advice that's commonly overlooked. You probably know someone incredibly productive and seemingly good with time management as long as their day goes according to plan. But they completely fall apart when that plan gets disrupted. This happens because they're inflexible.

Flexibility is largely unrecognized as a tool or trait that supports time management. But in my opinion, it is crucial because our schedules, plans, and routines are ultimately vulnerable to factors beyond our control. Moreover, flexibility is universally helpful since life occasionally throws curveballs at all of us.

PART V

BONUS SECTION: TIME MANAGEMENT FOR REMOTE WORKERS

~

Remote workers enjoy a lot of perks. But they also grapple with unique time management challenges. They have neither bosses nor coworkers to look over their shoulders, subtly compelling them to stay on track. They must rely on their initiative to properly manage their time.

Initially, this seems like a boon since less scrutiny equals more freedom. Less supervision equals more independence. But over time, the lack of oversight can erode the remote worker's discipline and sense of accountability. Once these two things vanish, remaining productive and efficient becomes much more challenging.

If you're a remote worker, this section is for you. It

speaks directly to your unique issues in managing your time. By its end, you'll possess the tools you need to get things done regardless of the environment in which you work.

HOW TO MAXIMIZE YOUR TIME WHEN WORKING REMOTELY

⁓

The time management tips we'll cover below are applicable whether you work in a typical office environment or remotely. But they're doubly important in the latter case. You alone are in charge of how you use your time. This means you alone are responsible for how effectively you put it to use.

Whether you work from home, at a local coffee house or library, or while on the road, working remotely can be both liberating and stressful. You enjoy more flexibility but must also deal with more distractions. You have more autonomy but may also experience less motivation and willpower. You might find it easier to work without interruptions but more challenging to remain disciplined.

The following tips will ensure that you stay on course. A few will seem intuitive. But don't discount them.

Together they'll help you to manage your time, stay productive, and complete the tasks and projects that are most important to you.

Designate Work-Only Spaces

If you mainly work from home, it's easy to set up shop wherever you're comfortable. You might work in your kitchen while eating breakfast, migrate to your living room for a few hours, and end up in your bedroom during the afternoon.

The problem is that working wherever you feel like working introduces distractions, such as your television, refrigerator, and neighbors (if you work on your porch). It also blurs the lines between your professional and personal lives, potentially upsetting your work-life balance.

To avoid these issues, choose a location in your home and designate it as a work-only space. Steer clear of this space whenever you're not working. When you need to work, you'll find it easier to concentrate and stay in "work" mode.

Schedule Breaks

The most reliable truism about breaks is that you probably won't take them if you don't schedule them. It's easy to get trapped in the mindset that staying productive requires that you continue to work.

Research shows that the opposite effect occurs.[1] After a

certain point (45 to 60 minutes), the longer we work without taking a break, the less we can focus. As our focus declines, so too does our awareness and performance.

Bottom line: schedule your breaks. Put them on your calendar so they'll become a part of your routine. Don't feel guilty about taking them. Instead, remind yourself that taking breaks improves your productivity.

Block Social Media

Social media can often feel like an addiction. We visit Facebook, Twitter, and Instagram over and over throughout the day, enjoying the accompanying dopamine rush. However, each time we do so, we surrender our focus and break our flow.

While some addictions may be beneficial (I'm looking at you, caffeine), social media isn't one of them. It's a distraction. The worst part is that it's a constantly updated distraction. Social media delivers endless stimulation that results in a continual dopamine rush.

Block social media while you're working. If you struggle to ignore sites like Facebook and Twitter, consider using a site blocker.[2] You can always surf these sites during your breaks.

Set Boundaries (For Others and Yourself)

Setting boundaries is vital regardless of where you work. They help you to stay focused and in flow. They also defend you against unnecessary interruptions, protecting your time from those who might otherwise squander it. An example is letting coworkers know you'll be unavailable on weekends.

Boundaries also protect us from ourselves. We give ourselves less latitude to waste time by imposing them. For example, you might refrain from social media until after lunch. This is a self-imposed boundary that will help you to stay on track while you work.

People often neglect to set and communicate their boundaries, trusting coworkers, friends, family members, and neighbors will intuit their priorities. But this rarely works. Setting boundaries and directly informing others about them is far more effective.

One last note: You will undoubtedly encounter people who repeatedly cross your boundaries. Be prepared for this circumstance. Know in advance how you'll address it, including what you'll say to the individual to discourage their boundary-crossing in the future. Whenever possible, approach the situation with compassion and grace rather than anger.

Avoid Personal Tasks during Your Workday

This tip might seem contentious. After all, what's the point of enjoying freedom and independence as a remote worker if you can't use them to get personal items done? It's a fair question.

The problem is that working on personal to-do items

during the workday prevents you from focusing on the work related to your job. It can also become a rationalization for procrastination.

For example, suppose you're at home preparing a sales presentation. Suddenly you remember that you need to do laundry. So you spend a few minutes prepping the loads and getting them started. Then you realize that there are unwashed dishes in your sink. So you attend to them, too. Next, you recall that you need to pay a few bills. Since they're on your mind, you decide to do that in the present.

Before long, the single personal item that grabbed your attention (laundry) has become a series of tasks. You're no longer focused on the work you need to complete for your job. And you may be now using these personal items to delay getting back to work.

If personal tasks grab your attention during the workday, write them on a to-do list. Wait until you take a break to address them. Or wait until you've called it quits for the day. That's a good segue into the final tip for managing your time while working remotely.

Set a Quitting Time and Uphold It

When you work in an office, it's easy to know when to call it a day. There's something about the environment that encourages you to stick to a routine. When the clock hits 5:00 p.m., it's time to pack up and head home.

When you work remotely, quitting time is less clear. It's sometimes difficult to stop working, especially if you've reached a flow state. This is doubly true when there's no clear distinction between areas in your home designated for work and areas designated for leisure.

I used to find myself working past 2:00 a.m regularly. Why? First, there was always more work to do than the time available to do it. This is the essence of time management, and I'm chagrined to admit I was terrible at it back then.

Second, I didn't have a compelling reason to stop working. I wasn't married then, so keeping my nose to the grindstone was easy. Additionally, I didn't prioritize my mental and emotional well-being, figuring (incorrectly) that they would take care of themselves.

Third, I neglected to set a personal boundary that governed when I would and wouldn't work. This was a crucial oversight. Combined with my tendency to burn the midnight oil, it predictably led to burnout. My stress levels went through the roof. My social life evaporated. And I was constantly irritable, exhausted, and unhappy.

So I made a change: I set a quitting time. No longer would I work after 6:00 p.m. No longer would I grind into the morning hours.

An unexpected outcome resulted. I got *more* work done. With a 6:00 p.m. quitting time, I stopped wasting so much time during the day. I stuck to my schedule, used time blocks, and applied Parkinson's law to every task and project. I became more productive and much better at managing my time.

If you don't currently have a quitting time, I strongly

encourage you to set one. Test different parameters and note the ones that best suit your circumstances. You can set times for specific days of the week. Or set different times for Monday through Friday and the weekend (if you work on weekends).

This is a simple tip that remote workers often overlook. But it can be an absolute game changer in your life. It will not only improve your time management skills, but it will also help you to find and maintain a healthy work-life balance.

And that might be the biggest reward of all.

---

1. Ariga, Atsunori and Lleras, Alejandro (2011, March) Brief and rare mental "breaks" keep you focused: deactivation and reactivation of task goals preempt vigilance decrements. *Cognition*, 118(3), pages 439-443, https://doi.org/10.1016/j.cognition.2010.12.007
2. I recommend the app Freedom which can be found at https://freedom.to/.

FINAL THOUGHTS ON THE TIME
MANAGEMENT SOLUTION

~

We've finally crossed the finish line. You now possess the tools to optimize your time management and increase productivity. But I'd like to leave you with a few last thoughts to consider.

First, remember that there is no perfect time management system. At the beginning of our journey, I made the point, and it's important enough to reiterate here. We've covered many tactics and strategies to help you manage your time. But don't think of them as rules. Don't even think of them as guidelines. The fact is that they won't work for everyone. All of us have unique circumstances.

Instead, please consider the tactics and strategies we've covered throughout this book as *suggestions*. Test them. Put each one through its paces. Then, record the results. If a particular tip works for you, fantastic! Implement it. If not, ignore it. That's fine, too.

The goal of *The Time Management Solution* was never to get you to fall in love with a specific system. I intended to present every tactic I've used with success and then encourage you to try them. You'd gradually put together a tailor-made time management system that suits you by testing each and noting the results.

The second thought I'd like to leave you with concerns how you adopt your new time management system. I believe the best way to make lasting changes in our lives is to take small steps forward. Rather than making a radical, comprehensive transformation all at once, make small adjustments.

In the context of what we've covered in *The Time Management Solution*, this means focusing on one tactic at a time. Spend a few days testing it. Note whether it aligns with your circumstances. Don't rush the process by adopting several in one go. It's like visiting a terrific all-you-can-eat buffet. Instead of wolfing it all down, take the time to savor each item. If you like something, go back for seconds.

Lastly, this book is organized so you can return to it repeatedly. If you need a refresher on prioritizing your to-do list, revisit Tactic #3. If you'd like to remind yourself of the finer details regarding Parkinson's law, reread Tactic #14. Or, if time again starts slipping through your fingers, take another glance through Section 2 to check whether you're making common mistakes.

The Time Management Solution can pay dividends for many years to come. Congratulations on completing the journey. I'm excited for you, and I encourage you to revisit as your needs require.

Onward.

DID YOU ENJOY READING THE TIME MANAGEMENT SOLUTION?

~

Thank you for reading *The Time Management Solution*. I know your time's importance, so I greatly appreciate your decision to spend some of it with me. It is my sincere hope that you feel the time was well spent.

If you found this book helpful, would you consider leaving a review on Amazon? It doesn't need to be long. One or two short sentences about a tip or section you liked would be perfect. It would mean the world to me. Plus, your review will encourage other folks to read this book.

One final note: I have several more books planned on various aspects of time management and productivity. If you'd like to be notified of when I release them (usually for less than $1 for a short time), consider joining my mailing list. You'll receive my 40-page PDF ebook titled *Catapult*

Your Productivity! The Top 10 Habits You Must Develop To Get More Things Done.
You can join my list at the following address:

http://artofproductivity.com/free-gift/

I'll also send you my best productivity and time management tips via my email newsletter. You'll receive tips and tactics on beating procrastination, creating morning routines, avoiding burnout, and developing razor-sharp focus, along with many other productivity hacks!

If you have questions or want to share a tip, technique, or mind hack that has made a positive difference in your life, please feel free to reach out to me at damon@artofproductivity.com. I'd love to hear about it!

Until next time,

Damon Zahariades
http://artofproductivity.com

ABOUT THE AUTHOR

Damon Zahariades is a corporate refugee who endured years of unnecessary meetings, drive-by chats with coworkers, and a distraction-laden work environment before striking out on his own. Today, in addition to writing a growing catalog of time management and productivity books, he's the showrunner for the productivity blog ArtofProductivity.com.

He enjoys playing chess, poker, and the occasional video game with friends in his spare time. And he continues to promise himself that he'll start playing the guitar again.

Damon lives in Southern California with his beautiful, supportive wife and their affectionate, quirky, and sometimes mischievous dog, Rocky. He's looking wistfully at his 50th birthday in the rearview mirror.

OTHER BOOKS BY DAMON ZAHARIADES

The Art of Letting GO

Finally, let go of your anger, regrets, and negative thoughts and enjoy the emotional freedom you deserve!

How to Make Better Decisions

Fourteen proven tactics to overcome indecision, consistently make intelligent choices, and create a rewarding life in the process!

The Mental Toughness Handbook

The definitive, step-by-step guide to developing mental toughness! Exercises included!

To-Do List Formula

Finally! Discover how to create to-do lists that work!

The Art Of Saying NO

Are you fed up with people taking you for granted? Learn how to set boundaries, stand your ground, and inspire others' respect in the process!

The Procrastination Cure

Discover how to take quick action, make fast decisions, and overcome your inner procrastinator!

Fast Focus

Here's a proven system that'll help you to ignore distractions, develop laser-sharp focus, and skyrocket your productivity!

The 30-Day Productivity Plan

Need a daily action plan to boost your productivity? This 30-day guide is the solution to your time management woes!

The 30-Day Productivity Plan - VOLUME II

30 MORE bad habits sabotaging your time management - and how to overcome them one day at a time!

The Time Chunking Method

It's one of the most popular time management strategies used today. Triple your productivity with this easy 10-step system.

80/20 Your Life!

Achieve more, create more, and enjoy more success. Here's how to get more done with less effort and change your life in the process!

Small Habits Revolution

Change your habits to transform your life. Use this simple, effective strategy for adopting any new habit you desire!

Morning Makeover

Imagine waking up excited, energized, and full of self-confidence. Here's how to create morning routines that lead to explosive success!

The Joy Of Imperfection

Finally, beat perfectionism, silence your inner critic, and overcome your fear of failure!

The P.R.I.M.E.R. Goal Setting Method

An elegant 6-step system for achieving extraordinary results in every area of your life!

Digital Detox

Disconnect to reconnect. Discover how to unplug and enjoy a more mindful, meaningful, and rewarding life!

For a complete list, please visit

http://artofproductivity.com/my-books/

Made in the USA
Las Vegas, NV
14 January 2023

65613730R00134